**THE ROYAL COURT
THEATRE PRESENTS**

UNIVERSITY OF
WINCHESTER

a profoundly affectionate, passionate devotion to someone *(-noun)*

by debbie tucker green

a profoundly affectionate
devotion to someone *(-n*
performed at the Royal Court
Upstairs, Sloane Square, on Tu
2017.

KA 0429809 8

a profoundly affectionate, passionate devotion to someone *(-noun)*

by debbie tucker green

CAST (in alphabetical order)

Man **Gary Beadle**
B **Gershwyn Eustache Jnr**
A **Lashana Lynch**
Young Woman **Shvorne Marks**
Woman **Meera Syal**

Written & directed by **debbie tucker green**
Designer **Merle Hensel**
Lighting Designer **Lee Curran**
Sound Designer **Christopher Shutt**
Movement Director **Vicki Manderson**
Assistant Director **Jade Lewis**
Casting Director **Amy Ball**
Production Manager **Marius Rønning**
Assistant Production Manager **Kate Jones**
Costume Supervisor **Sabrina Cuniberto**
Stage Managers **Lizzie Chapman, Charlotte Padgham**
Set Built by **Set Blue Scenery**

a profoundly affectionate, passionate devotion to someone *(-noun)*

by debbie tucker green

debbie tucker green (writer/director)

For the Royal Court: **hang, truth & reconciliation, random, stoning mary.**

Other theatre includes: **nut (National); generations (Young Vic); trade (RSC/RSC at Soho); born bad (Hampstead); dirty butterfly (Soho).**

Film and television includes: **second coming, random.**

Radio includes: **lament, gone, random, handprint, freefall.**

Directing includes: **hang, nut, truth & reconciliation (theatre); second coming (feature film); random (film); lament, gone, random (radio).**

Awards include: **Radio Academy Arias Gold Award (lament); International Film Festival Rotterdam Big Screen Award (second coming); BAFTA for Best Single Drama (random); Black International Film Award for Best UK Film (random); OBIE Special Citation Award (born bad, New York Soho Rep. production); Olivier Award for Most Promising Newcomer (born bad).**

Gary Beadle (Man)

For the Royal Court: **Sucker Punch, God's Second In Command.**

Other theatre includes: **Now We Are Here (Young Vic); Les Blancs, Black Poppies (National); Hapgood (Hampstead); The Whipping Man (Theatre Royal, Plymouth); The Rise & Shine of Comrade Fiasco (Gate); Skipping Rope, You Know Who You Are (Talawa), Banksy: The Room in the Elephant (Tobacco Factory/Edinburgh Festival Fringe/UK tour); Blue Remembered Hills (Chichester Festival); Family Man, Alterations (Theatre Royal Stratford East); Top Dog/Under Dog (Crucible, Sheffield); The Memory of Water (Watford Palace); Generations of the Dead in the Abyss of Coney Island Madness (Contact); Ticker Tape & V Signs (7:84); Welcome Home Jacko (BTC, New York); Moby Dick (Royal Exchange, Manchester); Club Mix (Riverside Studios).**

Television includes: **Silent Witness, Grantchester, Death In Paradise, The Interceptor, Doctors, Common Ground, Crime Stories, Hustle, Casualty, Kerrching, Holby City, EastEnders, Family Affairs, The Bill, Absolutely Fabulous, Born to Run, Glam Metal Detectives, Shall I Be Mother, Murphy's Mob, The Lenny Henry Show, Honeymoon, Just Like Mohicans, Club Mix, Radical Chambers, I Love Keith Allen, Making Out, Crying Game, Wail of the Banshee,** Space Virgins From Planet Sex Queen of the Wild, The Detectives.

Film includes: **In the Heart of the Sea, Cockneys vs Zombies, 'Til Death Us Do Part, Wit, The Imitators, Driven, Memoirs of a Survivor, Fords on Water, Absolute Beginners, Playing Away, Cresta Run, White Mischief.**

Lee Curran (Lighting Designer)

For the Royal Court: **X, Constellations (& West End/Broadway).**

Other theatre includes: **Splendour (Donmar); The Oresteia (Home, Manchester); Love's Sacrifice, Arden of Faversham (RSC); Hamlet, Much Ado About Nothing, Blindsided (Royal Exchange, Manchester); Mametz (National Theatre Wales); Protest Song (National); A Number (Nuffield); Regeneration, Dancing at Lughnasa (Royal & Derngate); Blam! (Neander); The Jungle Book (West Yorkshire Playhouse); Turfed, 66 minutes in Damascus (LIFT); The Sacred Flame (ETT/Rose Kingston); The Fat Girl Gets A Haircut & Other Stories, Puffball (Roundhouse) The Rise & Shine of Comrade Fiasco, Unbroken (Gate); Clytemnestra (Sherman Cymru); The Empty Quarter (Hampstead).**

Dance includes: **Sun, Political Mother, The Art of Not Looking Back, In Your Rooms, Uprising (Hofesh Schecter); Untouchable (Royal Ballet); Frames, Curious Conscience (Rambert); The Measures Taken, All That is Solid Melts into Air, The Grit in the Oyster (Alexandra Whitley); Bastard Amber, Interloper (Liz Roche); There We Have Been (James Cousins); Wide Awakening (Joss Arnott).**

Opera includes: **Orpheé et Eurydice (ROH); Nabucco (Opera National de lorraine); Ottone, Life On The Moon (English Touring Opera).**

Gershwyn Eustache Jnr (B)

Theatre includes: **The Royale (Bush); The Comedy of Errors, Macbeth on Film (Globe); Home, nut (National); Romeo & Juliet (Custom Practice/UK tour).**

Television includes: **Britannia, Fortitude, Legends, Peter Pan, Run, New Worlds.**

Film includes: **The Yellow Birds, Second Coming, Starred Up.**

Merle Hensel (Designer)

For the Royal Court: **X, The Mistress Contract.**

Other theatre includes: **Macbeth (Costumes only) (Young Vic); Arden of Faversham (RSC); Much Ado About Nothing (Royal Exchange, Manchester); Protest Song (National); Macbeth (National Theatre of Scotland / Lincoln Center / Broadway / Japanese Tour); Green Snake (National Theatre of China), 27, The Wheel (National Theatre of Scotland); Glasgow Girls (National Theatre of Scotland and Nationwide Tour); The Shawl, Parallel Elektra (Young Vic); Shun-Kin (Theatre de Complicite); The Girls Of Slender Means (Stellar Quines Theatre Company); Diener Zweier Herren (Schlosstheater Vienna); Ippolit (Sophiensaele, Berlin; Schauspielhaus Zürich; Münchner Kammerspiele); Der Verlorene (Sophiensaele, Berlin); Kupsch (Deutsches Theater, Göttingen).**

Opera includes: **Maria Stuarda (Vereinigte Bühnen, Mönchengladbach/Krefeld); Der Vetter Aus Dingsda (Oper Graz); Lunatics (Kunstfest Weimar); 'Münchhausen, Herr Der Lügen (Neuköllner Oper, Berlin).**

Dance includes: **Tenebre (Ballett am Rhein); The Barbarians In Love (Costumes only), Sun, Political Mother (Hofesh Schechter Company); Lovesong (Frantic Assembly); James Son Of James, The Bull, The Flowerbed (Fabulous Beast Dance Theatre); Justitia, Park (Jasmin Vardimon Dance Company); Human Shadows (Underground7; The Place Prize).**

Film includes: **Morituri Te Salutant, Baby.**

Merle Hensel works internationally in a wide variety of styles and genres. She also is a lecturer at Central St Martins School of Art and Design in London. Other teaching includes Rose Bruford College and Goldsmiths.

Jade Lewis (Assistant Director)

As director, theatre includes: **On The Edge of Me (Soho/Rich Mix).**

As movement director, theatre includes: **Followers (Southwark).**

As assistant director, theatre includes: **The Convert, Iphigenia Quartet (Gate); Madness Sweet Madness (Martin Harris, Manchester/Lantern, Liverpool); Venus/Mars (Old Red Lion/Bush).**

Jade was the Boris Karloff Trainee Assistant Director on Blackta by Nathaniel Martello-White at the Young Vic. She is currently a Creative Associate at The Gate Theatre and one of Ovalhouse's Emerging Artist team. She has also directed and assisted on community projects for Southwark Playhouse, Southbank Centre and The Young Vic.

Lashana Lynch (A)

Theatre includes: **Educating Rita (Chichester Festival Theatre); Roadkill (Pachamama); Romeo & Juliet (Royal National Theatre); Slave (Lowry Theatre); Some Like It Hip Hop (ZooNation/Sadler's Wells).**

Television includes: **Still Star-Crossed, Death in Paradise, Crims, Atlantis, Top Coppers, The 7:39, Silent Witness, Doctors, The Bill.**

Film includes: **Brotherhood, Fast Girls, Powder Room.**

Vicki Manderson (Movement Director)

As movement director for the Royal Court: **The Children.**

As associate movement director for the Royal Court: **The Twits, Let the Right One In (& National Theatre of Scotland/West End/St Ann's, New York). As movement director, theatre includes: Details (Grid Iron); Housed (Old Vic New Voices); Juicy & Delicious (National); The Silence of The Sea (Donmar).**

As associate movement director, other theatre includes: **In Time O' Strife, Black Watch (National Theatre of Scotland); The Curious Incident of the Dog in the Night-Time (National/West End). As Actor, theatre includes: In Time O' Strife, Knives in Hens, Beautiful Burnout (& Frantic Assembly), Home Inverness (National Theatre of Scotland); Dr Dee (ENO/Manchester International Festival); The Two Gentlemen of Verona (Royal & Derngate); (in)visible dancing, LOL, To the Bone (Protein Dance).**

Shvorne Marks (Young Woman)

Theatre includes: **Deny Deny Deny (Park); House (Clean Break/Yard); The Brink, Macbeth (Orange Tree); Flare Path (UK tour); The Witch of Edmonton (RSC); Some Other Mother (Traverse/Tron); Home (The Last Refuge); Trust Fund (Bush); Seasoned (Tobacco Factory).**

Television includes: **Endeavour, Holby City.**

Radio includes: **Assata Shakur.**

Christopher Shutt (Sound Designer)

For the Royal Court: **Escaped Alone, The Sewing Group, Love & Information (& New York), Kin, Aunt Dan & Lemon, Bliss, Free Outgoing, The Arsonists, Serious Money, Road.**

Other theatre includes: **Twelfth Night, Here We Go, The Beaux Stratagem, Man & Superman, The James Plays (I & II), From Morning to Midnight, Strange Interlude, Timon of Athens, The Last of the Haussmans, The White Guard, Burnt by the Sun, Every Good Boy Deserves Favour,**

The Hour We Knew Nothing of Each Other, War Horse (& West End), Philistines, Happy Days, Thérèse Raquin, The Seagull, Burn/Chatroom/Citizenship, Coram Boy, A Dream Play, A Minute Too Late, Measure for Measure, Mourning Becomes Elektra, Play Without Words, Machinal (National); St Joan, Faith Healer (Donmar); Wild (Hampstead); Merchant of Venice (Globe); The Entertainer, The Winter's Tale (West End); The Father (Theatre Royal, Bath/Tricycle/West End); Hamlet (Barbican); Bull (Young Vic); Privacy, The Same Deep Water As Me, Philadelphia, Here I Come!, Piaf, The Man Who Had All the Luck, Hecuba (Donmar); The Playboy of the Western World, All About My Mother, Life x 3 (Old Vic); Ruined, Judgement Day (Almeida); Desire Under the Elms, Blasted (Lyric, Hammersmith); A Human Being Died That Night, And No More Shall We Part, For Once (Hampstead); Thyestes (Arcola); Shoes (Sadler's Wells); The Caretaker (Crucible, Sheffield/Tricycle); Julius Caesar (Barbican); Oppenheimer (& West End), The Two Gentlemen of Verona, Wendy & Peter Pan, Candide, Twelfth Night, The Comedy of Errors, The Tempest, King Lear, Romeo & Juliet, Noughts & Crosses, King John, Much Ado About Nothing (RSC); Macbeth (Manchester International Festival/New York); Drum Belly (Abbey); Crave/4:48 Psychosis (Sheffield Theatres); Far Away, A Midsummer Night's Dream (Bristol Old Vic); Good (Royal Exchange, Manchester); Man of Aran (Druid, Galway); The House of Special Purpose (Chichester Festival); Little Otik, The Bacchae (National Theatre of Scotland); Riders to the Sea (ENO); A Disappearing Number, The Elephant Vanishes, Mnemonic, The Noise of Time, The Street of Crocodiles, The Three Lives of Lucie Cabrol, The Caucasian Chalk Circle (Complicite); A Human Being Died That Night, Macbeth, All My Sons, The Resistible Rise of Arturo Ui, Happy Days, A Moon for the Misbegotten, Coram Boy, Humble Boy, Not About Nightingales, Mnemonic (Broadway).

Awards include: **Tony Award for Best Sound Design of a Play (War Horse); Evening Standard Theatre Award (A Disappearing Number); New York Drama Desk Award for Outstanding Sound Design (Mnemonic, Not About Nightingales).**

Meera Syal (Woman)

For the Royal Court: **If You Don't Let Us Dream We Won't Let You Sleep, Serious Money (& West End/Broadway), The Great Celestial Cow, Minor Complications, True Dare Kiss, Byrthrite.**

Other theatre includes: **Romeo & Juliet (Kenneth Branagh/West End); Behind the Beautiful Forevers, Rafta Rafta, Peer Gynt (National); Much Ado About Nothing (RSC); The Killing of Sister George (Arts); Shirley Valentine (Menier/Trafalgar); Bombay Dreams (Really Useful/West End); The Vagina Monologues (Old Vic/West End/Broadway); One of Us (Edinburgh International Festival/Off-Broadway); Kissing God (Hampstead); Blood Wedding (Half Moon**

& UK Tour); The School for Scandal (Bristol Old Vic); Kirti Sona & Ba (Haymarket, Leicester); My Girl (Theatre Royal Stratford East); Goodness Gracious Me (UK tour).

Television includes: **Riviera, Walliams & Friends, The Musketeers, Midsomer Murders, Broadchurch, The Brink, The Boy in the Dress, Psychobitches, The Job Lot, The Kumars at No. 42, Crackanory, Silk, Bollywood Carmen, Family Tree, Hunted, Mr Swallow, The Jury, Doctor Who, Little Crackers, Jekyll, The Amazing Mrs Pritchard, The Secretary Who Stole £4 Million, Life Isn't All Ha Ha Hee Hee, Goodness Gracious Me, Who Do You Think You Are?, Linda Green, Fat Friends, Mrs Bradley Mysteries, Absolutely Fabulous, Sean's Show, Jo Brand's Through the Cakehole, My Sister Wife, Crossing the Floor, The Real McCoy, Kinsey, A Little Princess, Secret Diary of Adrian Mole.**

Film includes: **Murder on the Orient Express, Paddington 2, The Nutcracker & the Four Realms, Dr Strange, Alice Through the Looking Glass, Absolutely Anything, All in Good Time, You Will Meet a Tall Dark Stranger, Desert Flower, Mad Sad & Bad, Jhoom Barabar Jhoom, Scoop, Anita & Me, Girls Night, Beautiful Thing, It's Not Unusual, A Nice Arrangement, Sammy & Rosie Get Laid.**

Radio includes: **Small Town Murder, Bindi Business, Everyday Story of Afghan Folk, Leaving Normal, Kipling in Love, Verse Universe, Ladies Excuse Me, Poetry Please, Wicked Words, Morning Story, Book At Bedtime, Pankhiraj, Goodness Gracious Me.**

Awards include: **WhatsOnStage Award for Best Solo Performance (Shirley Valentine).**

THE ROYAL COURT THEATRE

The Royal Court Theatre is the writers' theatre. It is a leading force in world theatre for energetically cultivating writers – undiscovered, emerging and established.

Through the writers, the Royal Court is at the forefront of creating restless, alert, provocative theatre about now. We open our doors to the unheard voices and free thinkers that, through their writing, change our way of seeing.

Over 120,000 people visit the Royal Court in Sloane Square, London, each year and many thousands more see our work elsewhere through transfers to the West End and New York, UK and international tours, digital platforms, our residencies across London, and our site-specific work. Through all our work we strive to inspire audiences and influence future writers with radical thinking and provocative discussion.

The Royal Court's extensive development activity encompasses a diverse range of writers and artists and includes an ongoing programme of writers' attachments, readings, workshops and playwriting groups. Twenty years of the International Department's pioneering work around the world means the Royal Court has relationships with writers on every continent.

Within the past sixty years, John Osborne, Samuel Beckett, Arnold Wesker, Ann Jellicoe, Howard Brenton and David Hare have started their careers at the Court.

Many others including Caryl Churchill, Athol Fugard, Mark Ravenhill, Simon Stephens, debbie tucker green, Sarah Kane - and, more recently, Lucy Kirkwood, Nick Payne, Penelope Skinner and Alistair McDowall - have followed.

The Royal Court has produced many iconic plays from Laura Wade's **Posh** to Jez Butterworth's **Jerusalem** and Martin McDonagh's **Hangmen**.

Royal Court plays from every decade are now performed on stage and taught in classrooms and universities across the globe.

It is because of this commitment to the writer that we believe there is no more important theatre in the world than the Royal Court.

Supported using public funding by
ARTS COUNCIL ENGLAND

ROYAL

SPRING / SUMMER 2017

7 Mar – 8 Apr
Patrick Milling Smith, Barbara Broccoli, Robert Evans,
Michael G Wilson, Brian Carmody and the Royal Court Theatre
In association with Complicite

The Kid Stays in the Picture
Based on the life story of Robert Evans
Directed by Simon McBurney

19 Apr – 6 May
Nuclear War
Text by Simon Stephens
Directed by Imogen Knight

24 Apr – 20 May
Royal Court Theatre Productions, Sonia Friedman
Productions and Neal Street Productions

The Ferryman
By Jez Butterworth
Directed by Sam Mendes
West End transfer
20 Jun – 7 Oct, Gielgud Theatre

10 May – 20 May
MANWATCHING
By an anonymous woman

25 May – 24 Jun
Royal Court Theatre and Sherman
Theatre Cardiff
Killology
By Gary Owen
Directed by Rachel O'Riordan

3 Jun – 8 Jul
Anatomy of a Suicide
By Alice Birch
Directed by Katie Mitchell

5 Jul – 12 Aug
Bodies
By Vivienne Franzmann
Directed by Jude Christian

21 Jul – 9 Sep
Road
By Jim Cartwright
Directed by John Tiffany

Tickets from £12 0207 565 5000

royalcourttheatre.com

Supported using public funding by
**ARTS COUNCIL
ENGLAND**

ANATOMY OF A SUICIDE is part of the Royal Court's Jerwood
New Playwrights programme, supported by

JERWOOD **CHARITABLE**
FOUNDATION

Sloane Square London, SW1W 8AS
🐦 royalcourt 📘 royalcourttheatre
🚇 Sloane Square ⇌ Victoria Station

COURT

ROYAL COURT SUPPORTERS

The Royal Court is a registered charity and not-for-profit company. We need to raise £1.7 million every year in addition to our core grant from the Arts Council and our ticket income to achieve what we do.

We have significant and longstanding relationships with many generous organisations and individuals who provide vital support. Royal Court supporters enable us to remain the writers' theatre, find stories from everywhere and create theatre for everyone.

We can't do it without you.

PUBLIC FUNDING

Arts Council England, London
British Council

TRUSTS & FOUNDATIONS

The Bryan Adams Charitable Trust
The Austin & Hope Pilkington Trust
Martin Bowley Charitable Trust
Gerald Chapman Fund
CHK Charities
The City Bridge Trust
The Clifford Chance Foundation
Cockayne - Grants for the Arts
The Ernest Cook Trust
Cowley Charitable Trust
The Dorset Foundation
The Eranda Foundation
Lady Antonia Fraser for The Pinter Commission
Genesis Foundation
The Golden Bottle Trust
The Haberdashers' Company
The Paul Hamlyn Foundation
Roderick & Elizabeth Jack
Jerwood Charitable Foundation
Kirsh Foundation
The Mackintosh Foundation
Marina Kleinwort Trust
The Andrew Lloyd Webber Foundation
The London Community Foundation
John Lyon's Charity
Clare McIntyre's Bursary

The Andrew W. Mellon Foundation
The Mercers' Company
The Portrack Charitable Trust
The David & Elaine Potter Foundation
The Richard Radcliffe Charitable Trust
Rose Foundation
Royal Victoria Hall Foundation
The Sackler Trust
The Sobell Foundation
John Thaw Foundation
The Garfield Weston Foundation
The Wolfson Foundation

CORPORATE SPONSORS

AlixPartners
Aqua Financial Solutions Ltd
Bloomberg
Cadogan Estates
Colbert
Edwardian Hotels, London
Fever-Tree
Gedye & Sons
Kirkland & Ellis International LLP
Kudos
MAC
Room One
Sister Pictures

BUSINESS MEMBERS

Auerbach & Steele Opticians
CNC – Communications & Network Consulting
Cream
Hugo Boss UK
Lansons
Left Bank Pictures
Rockspring Property Investment Managers
Tetragon Financial Group
Vanity Fair

For more information or to become a foundation or business supporter contact Camilla Start: camillastart@ royalcourttheatre.com /020 7565 5064.

INDIVIDUAL SUPPORTERS

Artistic Director's Circle
Eric Abraham
Carolyn Bennett
Cas Donald
Lydia & Manfred Gorvy
Jack & Linda Keenan
Angelie & Shafin Moledina
Miles Morland
Anatol Orient
NoraLee & Jon Sedmak
Deborah Shaw
  & Stephen Marquardt
Jan & Michael Topham
Matthew & Sian Westerman
Mahdi Yahya

Writers' Circle
Mark & Charlotte Cunningham
Jane Featherstone
Piers & Melanie Gibson
Jean & David Grier
Luke Johnson
Mandeep Manku
Mr & Mrs Sandy Orr
Ian & Carol Sellars
The Wilhelm Helmut Trust
Anonymous

Directors' Circle
William & Asli Arah
Dr Kate Best
Katie Bradford
Chris & Alison Cabot
Richard Campbell-Breeden
Louis Greig
David Harding
Roderick & Elizabeth Jack
Melanie J Johnson
Nicola Kerr
Philip & Joan Kingsley
Emma Marsh
Rachel Mason
Andrew & Ariana Rodger
Anonymous (2)

Platinum Members
Moira Andreae
Nick Archdale
Michael Bennett
Clive & Helena Butler
Piers Butler
Gavin & Lesley Casey

Sarah & Philippe Chappatte
Michael & Arlene Cohrs
Clyde Cooper
Mr & Mrs Cross
Andrew & Amanda Cryer
Alison Davies
Matthew Dean
Sarah Denning
Cherry & Rob Dickins
Denise & Randolph Dumas
Robyn Durie
Mark & Sarah Evans
Sally & Giles Everist
Celeste & Peter Fenichel
Emily Fletcher
The Edwin Fox Foundation
Dominic & Claire Freemantle
Beverley Gee
Nick & Julie Gould
The Richard Grand Foundation
Jill Hackel & Andrzej Zarzycki
Carol Hall
Peter & Debbie Hargreaves
Sam & Caroline Haubold
Mr & Mrs Gordon Holmes
Damien Hyland
Trevor Ingman
Amanda & Chris Jennings
Ralph Kanter
Susanne Kapoor
David P Kaskel
  & Christopher A Teano
Vincent & Amanda Keaveny
Peter & Maria Kellner
Mr & Mrs Pawel Kisielewski
Rosemary Leith
Dr Ekaterina Malievskaia
  & George Goldsmith
Christopher Marek
  Rencki
Mrs Janet Martin
Andrew McIver
David & Elizabeth Miles
Barbara Minto
Siobhan Murphy
M. Murphy Altschuler
Peter & Maggie Murray-Smith
Ann & Gavin Neath CBE
Emma O'Donoghue
Georgia Oetker
Adam Oliver-Watkins
Crispin Osborne
Alexander Petalas
Andrea & Hilary Ponti
Greg & Karen Reid
Paul & Gill Robinson

Corinne Rooney
Sir Paul & Lady Ruddock
William & Hilary Russell
Sally & Anthony Salz
Antoinette Santamaria
Jane Scobie
Anita Scott
Bhags Sharma
Dr. Wendy Sigle
Andy Simpkin
Brian Smith
Taylor Smith
Mr John Soler
Maria Sukkar
Mrs Caroline Thomas
The Ulrich Family
Monica B Voldstad
Anne-Marie Williams
Sir Robert & Lady Wilson
Kate & Michael Yates
Anonymous (7)

With thanks to our Friends, Silver and Gold members whose support we greatly appreciate.

DEVELOPMENT COUNCIL

Majella Altschuler
Piers Butler
Chris Cabot
Sarah Chappatte
Cas Donald
Celeste Fenichel
Piers Gibson
Emma Marsh
Angelie Moledina
Anatol Orient
Andrew Rodger
Sian Westerman

For more information or to become a supporter please contact Charlotte Cole: charlottecole@royalcourttheatre.com/020 7565 5049.

Supported using public funding by
ARTS COUNCIL ENGLAND

Royal Court Theatre
Sloane Square,
London SW1W 8AS
Tel: 020 7565 5050
info@royalcourttheatre.com
www.royalcourttheatre.com

Artistic Director
Vicky Featherstone
Executive Producer
Lucy Davies

Associate Directors
Lucy Morrison, Hamish Pirie, John Tiffany, Graham Whybrow
Associate Designer
Chloe Lamford
Associate Playwright
Simon Stephens
Artistic Associates
Ola Animashawun, Chris Sonnex
Trainee Director
Grace Gummer‡

International Director
Elyse Dodgson
Associate Director (International)
Sam Pritchard
International Assistant
Sarah Murray

General Manager
Catherine Thornborrow
Assistant Producer
Minna Sharpe
Projects Producer
Chris James
Assistant to the Executive
Antonia Salib
Trainee Administrators
Romina Leiva Ahearne, Omar Phillips §

Young Court Manager
Romana Flello
Young Court Assistant
Maia Clarke
Young Court Workshops & Projects Assistant
Ellie Fulcher

Literary Manager
Chris Campbell
Deputy Literary Manager
Louise Stephens
Literary Assistant
Adam Narat

Head of Casting
Amy Ball
Casting Assistant
Arthur Carrington

Head of Production
Marius Rønning
Company Manager
Joni Carter
Head of Lighting
Steven Binks
Deputy Head of Lighting
Jamie Spirito
Lighting Technicians
Jess Faulks, Matthew Harding
JTD Programmer & Operator
Catriona Carter
Head of Stage
Dan Lockett
Stage Chargehand
Lee Crimmen
Chargehand & Building Maintenance Technician
Matt Livesey
Head of Sound
David McSeveney
Sound Deputy
Emily Legg
Head of Costume
Lucy Walshaw
Wardrobe Manager
Gina Lee

Finance Director
Helen Perryer
Financial Controller
Damian Clements
Financial Administrator
Rosie Mortimer
Accounts Assistant
Sian Ruffles
Finance Trainee
Lewis Kupperblatt§

Head of Press & Publicity
Anoushka Warden
Press Assistant
Christopher Williams

Head of Marketing & Sales
Holly Conneely
Marketing Manager
Dion Wilson
Marketing Officer
Candace Chan
Marketing Trainee
Amy Archer–Williams§

Sales & Ticketing Manager
Farrar Hornby
Box Office Manager
Helen Corbett
Box Office Sales Assistants
Will Bourdillon*, Laura Duncanson, Joe Hodgson, Margaret Perry*

Development Director (maternity leave)
Rebecca Kendall
Development Director (maternity cover)
Liv Nilssen
Deputy Development Director
Lucy Buxton
Head of Individual Giving (maternity cover)
Charlotte Christesen
Development Manager (maternity leave)
Luciana Lawlor
Corporate & Events Manager
Nadia Vistisen
Development Officer
Camilla Start
Development Officer
Charlotte Cole
Development Trainee
Joshua Parr§

Theatre Manager (maternity leave)
Rachel Dudley
Theatre Manager (maternity cover)
Louise Glover
Front of House Manager
Adam Lawler
Duty House Managers
Flo Bourne, Elinor Keber
Cover Duty House Managers
Rhiannon Handy, Tristan Rogers
Bar & Kitchen Manager
Ali Christian
Deputy Bar & Kitchen Manager
Robert Smael
Assistant Bar & Kitchen Manager
Jared Thomas
Head Chef
David Adams
Bookshop Manager
Simon David
Bookshop Assistant
Anna Brindle*

Stage Door/Reception
Paul Lovegrove, Tiiu Mortley, Jane Wainwright

Thanks to all of our Ushers and Bar & Kitchen staff.

§ Posts supported by The Sackler Trust Trainee Scheme

‡The post of Trainee Director is supported by an anonymous donor.

* Part-time.

ENGLISH STAGE COMPANY
President
Dame Joan Plowright CBE

Honorary Council
Sir Richard Eyre CBE
Alan Grieve CBE
Phyllida Lloyd CBE
Martin Paisner CBE

Council Chairman
Anthony Burton CBE
Vice Chairman
Graham Devlin CBE
Members
Jennette Arnold OBE
Judy Daish
Sir David Green KCMG
Noma Dumezweni
Joyce Hytner OBE
Stephen Jeffreys
Emma Marsh
Roger Michell
James Midgley
Anita Scott
Lord Stewart Wood
Mahdi Yahya

"There are no spaces, no rooms in my opinion, with a greater legacy of fearlessness, truth and clarity than this space."
Simon Stephens, Playwright in Residence

The Royal Court invests in the future of the theatre, offering writers the support, time and resources to find their voices and tell their stories, asking the big questions and responding to the issues of the moment.

As a registered charity, the Royal Court relies on the generous support of individuals to seek out, develop and nurture new voices. Please join us in **Writing The Future** by donating today.

You can donate online at **royalcourttheatre.com/donate** or via our **donation box in the Bar & Kitchen.**

We can't do it without you.

To find out more about the different ways in which you can be involved, please contact Charlotte Cole on 020 7565 5049 or at charlottecole@royalcourttheatre.com

The English Stage Company at the Royal Court Theatre is a registered charity (No. 231242)

UNIVERSITY OF WINCHESTER
LIBRARY

UNIVERSITY OF WINCHESTER
LIBRARY

a profoundly affectionate, passionate devotion
to someone (– *noun*)

debbie tucker green

2

Characters

A, *female, Black*
B, *male, Black*

WOMAN, *Black or Asian*
MAN, *Black*

PART THREE

MAN, *same character from Part Two. Some years later.*
YOUNG WOMAN, *the daughter of A+B. Some years later.*

He is significantly older than her. The Young Woman is of legal age.

A forward slash / marks an overlapping point in the dialogue.

Words in brackets are intention only.

Names appearing without dialogue directly above/below each other indicate active silences between those characters listed.

A name appearing without dialogue indicates an active silence.

This text went to press before the end of rehearsals and so may differ slightly from the play as performed.

PART ONE

Scene One

A	So is it –
B	no.
A	Is it that / you're –
B	No it is / not.
A	so it's
B	there is no 'it's' it's nothing there's nothing
A	you're not –
B	no. Nothing. There isn't.

Beat.

A	My bad.
B	Yeh.
A	
B	
B	'My bad' – piss off.
A	I've always –
B	no you haven't.
A	
B	
B	It's not always all about you.
A	Well. It usually is. Isn't it.

Beat.

…So there is –

B	no there / isn't.
A	you're –
B	no
A	you have a –
B	(*quietly*) fuck / me.
A	something's not right
B	you're jumping / to –
A	something about you's not / right.
B	(*dry*) really? Right. Me. Right.
A	I'm just –
B	is it? Me. Right. (*dry*) My bad.

Beat.

You jump to conclusions. You always jump to – jumped to conclusions and wrong conclusions in leaps and fuckin bounds

A	I know / you.
B	come to conclusions where there aint none
A	I do know / you.
B	makin me make conclusions where there ent / one.
A	I do still know you.
B	Makin me *want* to make conclusions where there ent none to make, me makin them to make you feel better bout concluding there are conclusions, when there aint no conclusions to be had. Shit.
A	…You ent never said something just to make me feel better.
B	I ent lied to make you feel better / no.
A	When have you ever said something to me to make me feel / better?

B	I'm not gonna lie to you to make / you –
A	Something considerate to – something mindful – and I'm not talking bout your / lies.
B	you wanting me to say somethin to say anythin just so you can feel somethin – somethin good about y'self – no – and I don't lie –
A	thass one right there
B	and I won't say somethin just to say anything and lies ent got nuthin to do with what I do and don't say what I will and won't say what I won't and don't say – want to say and don't – to you.
A	I think –
B	*jump* to conclusions –
A	I think that –
B	jump to your conclusions.
A	I think that this is still about / me.
B	(You) get me nervous to say anything me not knowin how you'd 'conclude' about it wrongly
A	you're nervous of nothing.
B	Nervous of you
A	couldn't make you nervous of nuthin that you didn't wanna be nervous of even if I wanted to.
B	You wanted to.
A	…I did not
B	you tried to
A	I do not
B	you wanted to try to.
A	I did (not). I –. I… No.

Beat.

You've never been nervous of me.

B   Y'sound disappointed.

                Beat.

A   You've never been nervous of anything about me.

                And there are no conclusions jumped to. Nothin
                in fuckin 'leaps and bounds' thank you – nuthin
                needed to be jumped to regarding you as you're /
                quite –

B   Here we / go.

A   quite straightforward.

B   Here. We. / Go.

A   In a straightforward sort of way.

B   That the best you can do?

A   No.

A
B

B   …You didn't understand my complexity.

A   I think I / did.

B   You never did understand how complex I could /
                be.

A   I think I did. I think, there weren't much *to*
                understand – I understood what was
                understandable.

B

A   What was coherent.

B   You didn't try to understand.

A   I understood what was there to-sometimes – and
                this is with respect – sometimes you mistook –
                I felt you mistook, complexity, for… confusions.

B
A

A   You were confusing – could be confusing.

B	For you.
A	(*dry*) Hmm no – you were, a bag of confusion. Bags a contradiction, inconsistent –
B	if you weren't able / to –
A	confusing generally and sometimes-sometimes – you mistook 'confusion' for actual... crap (*gestures*) was a bit crap about you. Not complex. Shit crap. About you. Bags of it.
B	...You weren't able to support my / complex –
A	Bit of a fuck up bit of a crap fuck / up.
B	You didn't have it in / you to –
A	(A) bit self-indulgent.
B	Patience wasn't one of / your –
A	Well, very self- / indulgent.
B	compassion wasn't something you ever –
A	I was compassionate
B	you were condescending
A	I was more than compassionate
B	and I / knew –
A	you drained my compassion well dry
B	knew you didn't understand me
A	I was desert-like you got me-you drained me to a desert-like / state.
B	knowin you didn't understand want to understand never did understand me was quite an underwhelming experience. Generally.
A	I went from bein an oasis of understanding to an – and I understood your lack of complexity which pissed you off I was more than patient with you which pissed you off more and you knew I could read you better'n you knew yourself – and underwhelming?

B	(*dry*) With all due respect and all that.
A	'Underwhelming'?
B	Or am I not bein straightforward enough for / you?
A	After seein y'mouth never sayin what y'mind was thinkin for years –
B	thass depth
A	now you got the-the no iss not – thass not depth thass *boring*. Was your eyes sayin one thing and your mouth not havin the bottle to follow / through.
B	Thass knowin you won't get what I got to say you won't have the patience compassion or complexity –
A	you were / boring.
B	so I didn't bother sayin it.
A	You were borin.
B	Don't bother sayin it.
A	In all aspects.
B	'All aspects' – borin'?
A	All aspects.
B	Fuck off.

Beat.

	…Straightforward is good.
A	I'm sure it is. If you were that.
	…Do you miss me?
B	
A	Do you even –
B	you leapt and fuckin bounded…?
A	Do you miss –.

B

A

A   You miss me…?

           …Did you miss being… 'Underwhelmed'?

           About me.
           At all.
           Then?

B   …

Scene Two

A *is busy*.

B   I want you. Yeah.
           I want you to me. Want you with me want me us.
           I want you beyond what I can say
           beyond what I got words for
           beyond my vocabulary
           beyond any vocabulary
           beyond language
           beyond imagination,
           beyond what words can do beyond what my
           words can do. Beyond what words have been
           known to do, have yet to do, beyond what they
           will ever do.
           I wanted you beyond sentence in between
           syllables above vowels under consonants and
           after punctuation.

           A *is busy*.

           And.
           Getting up aint gettin up when you ent got up
           with me.

           A *is busy*.

           No. And
           gettin up is like I never got up once when I wake
           up and get up with you, or-or if you-you aint yet
           got up and still lying by my side –

A   *what?*

B   But.

A   What?!

B   Not gettin up and layin by you with you on you
           too hot next to you, too cold far from you, lookin
           at my favourite bit.
           Of you.
           Breathing on my favourite bit.
           Of you.
           Touchin it. A bit. That bit. Of you. Just. Soft like –

A	I feel / it –
B	so soft you don't even know it
A	I know / it.
B	too soft for you to even feel / it.
A	I know it. Knew it. Felt it.
B	And-and you taste better'n my food ever did. And
A	seriously?
B	But.
A	God.
B	But my days-our days seemed shorter with you in em, you shortened the hours, made minutes not matter and seconds seem shit, racing to build our old age together. Days couldn't be long enough with you in em and nights was like blinkin before daylight dawned quick –
A	this is –
B	you was my –
A	(This) is a real revelation –
B	yeh you / was.
A	(you) never said you wanted me that much –
B	I –
A	never said none of this-this poetical... *shit* –
B	shit?
A	Then.
B	'Shit'?
A	That you seem to find so easy to say now.
B	'...Shit'?
A	(*dry*) Hmm. Yeh. *Shit*.
	Beat.

B	You liked it.
A	I never said I liked / it.
B	You never said you never liked / it.
A	I tolerated it and then just blocked it. Blocked it off blocked it out. Turned up the TV faked a phone call or somethin... Y'know.
A	
B	
B	...I didn't have to say...
A	
B	how much I... Shouldn't have to say, how much I...

(I) showed it instead.

Didn't stop showin you.
Did I?
Couldn't stop showin you.
Could I.
Wouldn't stop. Would I.

Thass how you did know – do know.
You did know. You did know you did know, you knew how much...? How much I...
Don't you?

Didn't you?

Scene Three

A	…When you do that thing…
B	
A	…When you do that-did that (thing), that you do – did. With your thing. To me –
B	with you.
A	That you did a lot, to me –.
B	With you.
A	Thinking I liked / it.
B	You liked it you did like me doin / it.
A	When you did that – kept doin / that
B	That thing that you liked
A	I didn't.
B	
A	Like it.
B	
A	I didn't like it.
B	…You didn't say you didn't like / it.
A	I never liked it.
B	You never said you never did like it.
A	I –
B	ever. Never. Not once. You never said that.

Beat.

You looked like you liked it.

Beat.

You sounded like you liked / it.

A	What does that look look like then?

B   You made that sound that you made – that sound
         you make when you like – when you like it.
         While I was doin / it.

A   How did I sound then?

B   You know how you sounded. The sounds you-you
         – givin the looks you looked never sayin nothin
         bout not likin (nothin) – *I* didn't particularly like
         doin it but done it cos I knew you liked it and
         wanted to-wanted you to, y'know… Something
         you liked that I could do you-give you – do with
         you doin it right. That you liked.
         Even though I didn't like doin it. Selfless.
         Generous.

         Beat.
         Beat.

A   …That look that looks like I'm enjoying that
         thing that something you do – did – done back
         then… that look weren't that look that I liked it.
         It weren't that. And what you was doin you were
         doin cos you-you liked, *really* looked like you
         were enjoying doin more'n me –

B   that look weren't / that.

A   as you were doin it really *sounded* like you was
         enjoying doin it more'n / me –

B   That sound weren't / that.

A   while you was doin it

B   your looks weren't – and I-I dunno what your –
         and now you're lookin at me like… you're makin
         me unsure now – I dunno how you're-how you're
         looking at me now – how do I take (that) – how
         do I take this – what's this look / now?

A   I'm not looking at / you.

B   What is that what is that then what is / that?

A   You're lookin at me.

B   I don't even know now where to even (look) or to
        let you look, let you even look at me or I should
        look at the floor or summink, is it that? Look at
        the floor or su'un in silence. I dunno what you –
        I know you, know what things meant to you,
        what that thing meant to you what / you –

A   Stop lookin at me.

B   What doin that thing –

A   stop lookin at / me.

B   me doin that thing *with* you, meant to you and
        know I know that you liked it – what you look
        like when you liked it what you liking that thing
        looks like. I know.

        Beat.

        I do know.

        You did.
        …You did.

        Fuck.

Scene Four

A	When she looks at me (and) she looks at me, I see you I see you I – it's the weirdest thing / that –
B	It's great.
A	It is great – in the great way she looks at / me.
B	She looks at you a lot
A	(I) love lookin at her
B	I love lookin at her, it's great, love lookin at you
A	she's lovely to look at
B	still love lookin at / you.
A	she's got your eyes –
B	thass great
A	you see that? Got that depth –
B	great
A	that you got, she got that same complexity behind her eyes that you got she got the same colour as well although they say eye colour don't settle for the first few / months.
B	She looks at you a lot. She looks at you loads.
A	They say it's smell as much as anything –
B	(she) don't stop lookin at you
A	their eyes can't focus yet that young, they / say.
B	won't stop lookin at / you.
A	She's lookin but not lookin I don't think, don't think iss lookin how we think about lookin –
B	I think she's looking.
A	I think it's scent
B	looking at you.

A	She looks at you.
B	She looks at me and sees it's not you and looks for / you.
A	She looks at you
B	she looks *for* you.
A	I… think it's the milk she's sensing – scenting, the breast milk, instinct – built in, amazin – senses and that, thass why she looks for me – I'm sayin 'looks' y'know what I mean lookin but not lookin how we would / look.
B	She looks over my shoulder. For you. She turns her head when I have her. For you. Tries to lift her head when I hold her, looking for / you.
A	That don't really mean –
B	I look at you.
A	…Right.
B	But you're busy lookin at her.
A	
B	'Instinct' and all that, aye?
A	
B	
B	Amazin. I instinctively look at you. …You instinctively look at her.

A goes to say something then doesn't.

A	It doesn't really mean anything at this stage at this age… She's fresh, still fresh, learning and-and… getting familiar in this world and with this world an' workin us out as parents as we're working her out as our daughter, it's a first for all / of us.
B	She is lookin for you.

A   And it's amazin.

B   She looks like you.

A   It's amazin lookin in her eyes.

B   She got your / eyes.

A   Lookin deep into her eyes deep in them eyes and
           seein... you – thass what's amazin. Thass what
           I'm seein. All you. Only you.
           Really.

           ...None a me in there at all.

           Really.

Scene Five

B	– no no no.
	Beat.
	It's not you.
	Beat.
	…It – y'know that?
A	
B	Y'know that / right?
A	Right.
	Beat.
B	Yeh?
A	…I know / that.
B	Right.
A	…It's just –
B	it's me y'know
A	right.
B	Me not you.
A	…Right.
	Beat.
	It's just –
B	iss nuthin about you wouldn't be nuthin about you. You're still as –.
A	
B	Yeah? As you always were. Are.
	Beat.
	To me, y'know you are. That don't change that hasn't… y'know?

A

B   Just-it's-that it aint… It's that it's…

           Beat

           …Starts to feel a bit… Y'know.

A
B

B   Y'know?

A   …No.

           Beat.

B   A bit… …By-the-numbers y'know?

           Beat.

A

           Beat.

B   A bit… goin-through-the-motions…
           Y'know?

A   …No.

B   And iss me iss not you

A

B   iss all me

A   you / said.

B   I don't want you to feel that –

A   yeh. No

B   I don't want you to feel nuthin like that – it's –
           but it is, starting to feel a / bit…

A   I don't feel it is.

           Beat.
           Beat.

           I don't feel like it is like that.

B	
A	With you.
B	
A	With you with / me.
B	Iss kinda like-sorta –. …'Cos we should do', not that 'we want to do'
A	I want to / do.
B	y'know? Which gets a bit –
A	I want to / do.
B	a bit y'know –
A	no
B	I get a bit y'know
A	no.
B	…Bored.
A	
A	
B	And iss me. It's not you.
A	
B	You're still as…
A	
B	Y'know?
A	…I –
B	but it is boring.

Beat.

A	I –. I… I'm not bored / though.
B	Kinda routine borin even the… is actually borin.
A	

UNIVERSITY OF WINCHESTER
LIBRARY

B	It actually is. You know, you do what you do –
A	I thought it wasn't me
B	no no no, iss not / you.
A	you said it wasn't / me.
B	Yeh iss not-no iss not – I do what I do as well thass what I'm sayin, it's on me I – y'know you're –. It's not you it's not you. It's not (you) it's not that.
A	
B	Anyhow. Y'know…
A	
B	

Beat.

A	Right.

…Are you tired?

B	Yeh.

No.

Well… no.

Beat.
Beat.

A	Are you tired of me?

Beat.

B	…Yeh. No.

Beat.

Well…

Scene Six

A   …After Mum.
         After my mum… And I thought there was no
         after. When. After that.
         After then.
         I thought you'd… I thought you would… I did.

B

A   But you didn't.

B
A

A   Did yer. You wasn't.

B

A   Was yer? You couldn't.

B

A   Could yer.

         Weren't yer?

B

A   And I shouldn't have to say. Have had to say –

B   you never said anything about –

A   I shouldn't have to say anything.

B   …Don't say. Then. Nuthin don't say nuthin.
         Again.

         Beat.

A   I can't –

B   don't say anything cos after that, after then, after
         your mum, you saying nothin was your new sayin
         somethin / except –

A   I wasn't able to say anything.

B   I can't know –

A   was I? Wasn't able / to –

B   except I can't know what I don't know. I really can't –

A   you knew what was / happening

B   you didn't speak.

A   You saw what was happening.

B   You didn't speak

A   I didn't speak

B   you didn't speak to me, wouldn't speak to / me.

A   in all your poetical bollocks with how well you think you know me you coulda picked up on what I was goin through – I *couldn't* / speak.

B   After that, after then –

A   I couldn't speak –

B   after your mum you –

A   which was obvious.
          To someone with a bit of sense.

B   Nuthin about you – nuthin about you's obvious. And I didn't know what this new you of not sayin nuthin / was.

A   A blind man could see what I was goin through.

B   A clue a hint a sign an indication about your non-verbals to help me / out.

A   I wasn't there to help you out

B   woulda helped me to help you out and you weren't there –

A   I wasn't able to be (*taps head*) –

B   you weren't there

A   and you were no help

B   you didn't give me / the –

A   you helped nothing –

B   you didn't give me the chance / to –

A   I wasn't there to give you chances. I wasn't able
             'to help you out'. I wasn't able. That was the
             point and you were no help are no help. Can't
             help. Couldn't help. Didn't help. Didju?

B

A

B   …When I tried to help / you –

A   You didn't try.

B   When I tried to help you –

A   you didn't try hard enough.

B   You said I couldn't help.

             Y'said that much.

             Before you stopped speakin. You told me I couldn't
             – told me I had no idea told me I couldn't imagine,
             insisted that I wouldn't-wouldn't get close couldn't
             get close couldn't get-get nowhere near close
             enough to know what you was…

A

B   I know what you was going through –.

A   You've never been through it.

B   I could see you were –. I was waiting to help –

A   'waiting'

B   you wouldn't let me help.

A   'Waiting'.

B   You stopped speaking.

A   I stopped speaking, to you.

B

A

       Beat.

B   …I stayed.

A   No / help.

B   You, mute or otherwise I stayed.

A

B

B   Creepin round the house in your silence I / stayed

A   I weren't mute I was silent

B   you weren't speaking to me

A   I couldn't speak to / you.

B   just mute with me, quiet with me, silent with me. (*dry*) Nice.

A

B   And I talked to you.

A   You talked at me.

B   I talked to you – you not talkin back was your choice, talked to you through – talked you through – never stopped talkin never stopped tryin. (I) stepped up stepped in stepped to, even when you wouldn't let / me.

A   What you was sayin was wrong.

B   You dint let me / know.

A   What you was sayin weren't workin.

B   You could have let me know cos ten months of your bein mute –

A   I weren't / mute.

B   you bein morose

A   I was / in –

B   you bein fuckin miserable your fuckin silent way,
           got a bit grinding. You could have let me know
           sooner what I was sayin weren't workin coulda
           dropped a hint so I coulda saved my time saved
           my effort saved my tryin and saved my breath.

           Ten months. Ten months of it: forty weeks three
           hundred and seven days and nights of it. Of silent
           you – and those nights...

           He shakes his head. Says nothing else.

           (*quietly*) Fuck me.

           Beat.

           I more than know you.

           Beat.

           Ten months of you sayin nuthin to me when I dried
           your tears and your tears.
           And your tears.
           When I fed you healthy
           when I watched you not sleep.
           When I rubbed your aches and set your baths
           when I dried your body and lay you down
           then watched you not sleep more.
           When I dressed you-undressed you, combed out
           your hair, oiled your hair creamed your skin and
           (I) didn't touch you when I wanted to and I wanted
           to – when I wanted you
           and I wanted you.
           When I sat with you
           when I excused you
           when I drove you – walked you, walked with you
           stood by you and when I tried to fill the gaps your
           gaps with sayin somethin with sayin anything
           tryin to fill you up with what little I had to offer
           with what I had left to give and now you're tellin
           me that was all wrong? That that was all no good
           that weren't what you wanted weren't what you

needed and weren't a piece of it right or done
right anyway – and that I was the 'let down'?
Really?

Really?

Beat.

Fuck.

Beat.

Y'know…

He watches her.

Is this straightforward enough for you am I bein
straightforward enough for you – after your mum.
After that. After *then*.
Or am I bein confusing?

Cos, no.
No.

I don't miss that. About you.

At all.

Scene Seven

A	When I'm watching something…
B	
A	You listening?
B	Yeah.

He is not listening.

A	When I'm watching something, I am watching something. I am watching it. It's not just 'on'.
B	
A	You / listening?
B	Yeah.

He is not.

A   I don't just put it on. I'm not you, not you like that. I don't just put it on and leave it and leave it on and not watch it. If I put it on I'm watching it. I'm relaxing – trying to relax. You walk into the room – you walk in and it stops bein – I get – you walk in and I'm already distracted wondering how long I've got, how long till you start talkin or frapsin or looking for the remote or asking for the remote, or askin the kids for the remote or askin the kids to look for the remote – askin the kids to ask me for the remote cos I aint answered you, when I am still watchin – still trying to watch, halfway through – partway through my programme.

Beat.

Y'know?

Beat.

Are you / listening – ?

B	Yeh.

He's not listening.

A   And iss not right that I should have to – not that
      I do – but it's not normal to hide the remote –
      want to hide the remote, in your own house. Just
      so you can get through a programme.
      See you lookin, noisy lookin knowin you won't
      find it but the vibe is already – you've already
      mashed up the – talkin loud so I can't hear – well
      not the kids cos they know, but you, really talkin
      loud askin loud where it's at so I get distracted –
      thinkin iss funny I get distracted, when all I'm
      doin wanna do is watch my one programme
      without no interruptions. Y'know?

B

A   You lissenin?

B   Yeah.

      He is not.
      Beat.

A   Y'know?

B   …Yeah.

A   …Yeah.

      Cos that's not relaxing.

      Thass not relaxin.

      Beat.

      At all.

Scene Eight

They watch each other.

A   …That bit you can't see that bit you can't see of yourself… thass mine of you that bit-a-you-there that last nook of your neck that no one normally – that / bit.

B   The back of your right thigh –

A   that back-of-the-neck-bit there for me to-to remind you of / me –

B   no disrespect to the back of your left thigh but the back of your right thigh is mine.

A   When your head's down and they think they've bowed you tested you but not able to bruk you that piece of you is mine that part of you is all (mine)

B   sometimes I look down – head down deliberate not nuthin that they've done, not nuthin they could do but just enough just waiting for you, to have your feel just to have your touch just to have you on your favourite part a me there.

A
B

B   Sometimes I do that. Did that.

A   Miss that.

B   Do that. Still.

Scene Nine

B	He's perfect
A	he is perfect
B	ten fingers ten toes
A	juss like his dad
B	thank you
A	don't thank me it's us
B	it's you
A	took us to make / him
B	twenty-two hours of labour is all you
A	well, twenty-seven if we're counting.
B	You did / it.
A	He's perfect
B	he is perfect.
A	He's worth it. She'll love him
B	she'll love bein a big sis
A	even though she didn't want a brother.
B	She's got a brother she'll love him.
A	Even though she said clearly she didn't want no brother being brought home.
B	She will love / him.
A	She'll look at him / and –
B	She'll take one look and fall into these eyes of his.
A	She'll make a great, big sis
B	you're a great mum
A	(*dry*) you're an okay dad

B   and he's a beautiful boy already.

Thank you yeah.

Thank you.

Scene Ten

A	Lock it then –
B	what I'm sayin / is –
A	lock the door then
B	there isn't a lock on the door.
A	Put the lock on the door – you been sayin you was gonna do that for ages been sayin that for / years.
B	All I'm sayin is that / sometimes –
A	If you want one put one on
B	sometimes it would be –
A	if you want to put one on then I'll know –
B	sometimes I'd just like / to –
A	then we'll all know not to – when not to disturb you.
B	Sometimes, I'd just like to tek time to take a shit on my own is all / I'm –
A	So the kids know not to disturb Daddy
B	it's not even nice it's not even –
A	you come in when I'm on / the –
B	I leave if you're havin a shit.
A	Thass cos you're funny like that. If I have to come in –
B	no one has to come in then
A	if the kids need to come / in –
B	there's nothing the kids need enough bad enough to have to come in for the two minutes it takes / me –
A	it's not two minutes
B	takes me to have a –

A	it's never two / minutes
B	takes me to have a solitary shit. How is that –
A	if you –
B	how is that too much to ask?
A	If you wanna fit something fit an extractor fan. Stop you stinkin out the / place.
B	How is asking to have a – too much to fuckin…? I don't even know why I'm askin. Don't come in.
A	You're tellin me?
B	Don't come in when I'm takin a dump.
A	(*dry*) Very commanding.
B	How is this even / a – ?
A	You tellin me where I can and can't go in our own house / now?
B	It's a bathroom. I'm on the bog. Don't come / in.
A	I'll go where I like
B	I want some privacy.
A	I'll go where I / like.
B	I want some privacy when I –
A	I'd like some privacy when I'm getting undressed.
B	What?
A	In the bedroom when I'm – I've always hated getting undressed in front of / you.
B	*What?*
A	At night –
B	where did –
A	in the bedroom –
B	where did this –

A	at the end of the day –
B	where did this come from and thass different.
A	Feels like I'm bein judged.
B	I don't judge / you.
A	Feels like –
B	I've never judged (you) and you've always got undressed in front a me
A	always felt judged.
B	It's a bedroom.
A	Don't come in.
B	It's our bedroom.
A	It's our bathroom
B	you're not taking a shit
A	it's uncomfortable. I'm uncomfortable.
B	No you're not
A	always been uncomfortable
B	no you haven't
A	it's always uncomfortable getting undressed in front of you. Put a lock on the bathroom door I'll get changed in there.
A	
B	
B	…I don't make you feel uncomfortable…
A	
B	I make you feel (uncomfortable)…? You're not – you're not. You're…
A	
B	Are you?

Scene Eleven

A	– no no no.
	It's not you. …It – y'know that?
B	
A	Y'do know that right?
	Beat.
B	…It's just –
A	it's me y'know.
B	Right.
A	It is me not you.
B	…Right.
	It is just / that –
A	Iss nuthin about you wouldn't be nuthin about you. You're still as – as you ever were, as you always are. Y'know y'that.
	Beat.
B	
A	It's just, that it's… that it aint… It's that it's… starts to feel a bit. Y'know?
B	
A	A bit… By-the-numbers y'know?
B	
A	A bit goin-through-the-motions a bit routine… if you get what I / mean?
B	No
A	y'know?
B	…No.
A	And iss me iss not you, it is all me.
B	

UNIVERSITY OF WINCHESTER
LIBRARY

A	And I don't want you to feel that –
B	yeh. No.
	I don't feel that it's like that.
A	
B	With you.
A	
B	With you with / me.
A	It's feelin like we, that we sorta 'we should do' in a routine sorta-sorta – tedious sorta – y'know –
B	no
A	not that 'we want to do'
B	I want to / do.
A	which gets a bit –
B	I want to / do.
A	can get a bit y'know –
B	I / want –
A	I get a bit y'know. Bored.
B	
A	And it is me. It's not you.
	But. It is boring.
B	I –. I'm not / bored –
A	Kinda routine kinda borin even the doin it different... is actually borin.
B	
A	It actually is. Ennit?
B	

A	Isn't it?
B	
	(*quietly*) No. I –
A	y'know, you do what you / do –
B	you said it wasn't me.
A	Yeh iss not-no iss not it's not you – I do what I do as well it's as much me I – y'know you're –. It's not you, it's not you. It's not that.
	Anyhow.
B	Are you…
A	
B	…Are you tired of me?
A	You? No. …Yeh. No.
	Beat.
	Well…

Scene Twelve

B	How is it –
A	piss off.
	Beat.
B	How is it that it's only / your –
A	Piss off *really*
B	only your decision when I'm the
A	do I really need to / explain?
B	I'm the – and I do have a say –
A	you have a / say.
B	I should have a say –
A	you do have a say I'm lissenin to your say – again – you've said your say – again and you're still sayin it.
B	You're not listenin
A	I've heard it
B	but you're not / *lissenin.*
A	I've only got one way to listen –
B	which is the / problem.
A	two ears and whatever shit you're sayin reachin them.
B	You lissen closed you are closed. I lissen to you
A	nuthin about me's / closed.
B	have always lissened to you and you've always been closed
A	been too open to your / bullshit.
B	I listen to you
A	you talk over / me.
B	I lissen open to you and have to talk over you to be heard.

A   I've heard you. And I disagree. But, generously, I'm still listening to what you're sayin but you're always sayin it so I can't act surprised every time I hear / it.

B   You're not changing your mind.

A   I *hear* you, but, you're still talkin shit. You sayin what you're constantly sayin, again, don't mean I'ma change my mind bout this but-so as I've said, I've heard your say, heard you say so much I'm bored a fuckin hearin it and I do 'know who you are' and I hear that this shit seems 'unfair' but I'm not changing my (mind) you're not changing my (mind) you haven't never yet bout nuthin and y'won't about this, and if you actually heard what I been sayin –

B   what you're 'actually' sayin don't make no / sense.

A   *lissened* to why I'm sayin what I'm sayin –

B   what you're sayin is wicked.

A   Hear-wot. This ent no fifty-fifty I've heard your twenty per cent and my eighty per cent is still sayin the same consistent 'no' – and 'wicked'?

B   Spiteful and wicked

A   piss / off

B   I'm a good dad

A   'spiteful' – piss / off

B   I'm a great dad

A   'you're a great dad' I'm a great mum – or a 'spiteful and wicked' mum accordin to / you.

B   A spiteful and wicked wife – a good mum

A   but not a great one? Only you thass got the greatness is it? (I'm) not as great a parent as you is it?

B

A

A   (You) fuckin wish.

B   …One more.

A   No.

B   Just one / more.

A   We've got the set, boy and girl.

B   Two boys one girl –

A   no

B   two girls and a brother in between

A   no

B   I've always wanted three –

A   can't always get what we want

B   always said to you / three.

A   can't always get what we ask for.
           Can we.

           Beat.

B   …You're a / fuckin –

A   Hard horrible pregnancies

B   control freak / fuckin –

A   horrendous for months

B   bein a fuckin bitch –

A   distressing awful labour for days

B   fuckin bitch of a wife with how you're carryin on.

A
B

A   Nice.
           Nice.

B   Fuck you.

A   Well, no actually, seein as we're not tryin for
             another one –

B   cunt.

             Beat.

A
B
A
B

A   …Nice.

             Thank you.

             Thank you.

             For that.

Scene Thirteen

A	You know she needs talkin to.
B	
A	You know she needs you to talk (to) – she needs you talkin to – she needs to be able to talk to / you.
B	She can talk to me.
A	She wants to talk to / you.
B	She can talk to me I'm easy to talk to.

Beat.

A	She's not talkin.
B	Got somethin of her mum about her then.

Beat.

A	…That was different.
B	After your mother –
A	that was different
B	and so after her mother… she's not speaking. Sound familiar?
A	Thass not fair
B	not a lot fuckin is.
A	…She cries most nights you know that?
B	Then she's crying over you.
A	She is crying over me but you're still / here.
B	If she wants to cry over / you –
A	And it is most nights
B	that's up to her.
A	It's most every night
B	if she wants to cry over you and doesn't want to come to me / then –

A	she wants to come to you. But you don't hear that, you don't hear her over your TV the crap TV you have on loud too loud so loud or the crap radio thatchu you have on so loud too loud and then turn up, you don't hear her over that do yer?
B	I miss turning over your crap programmes.
A	She needs you.
B	I miss makin noise lookin for the remote halfway through what you was watchin –
A	she needs you to talk to her.
B	Don't hear her crying over my tears.
A	You're the adult.
B	
A	
B	She hasn't cried since your service.
A	Which was a shit service – I left instructions
B	that didn't make any sense
A	easy to follow easy for you to follow deliberately easy to follow to avoid you messin it up – which you did. It was a shit / service.
B	I weren't playing what you wanted played at your / service.
A	I'd written down what I wanted
B	we weren't playin that tacky – no, we would have had to sit through it and lissen to it and remember that – so / no.
A	It was my last wish and this isn't the point she's –
B	that would give her something to cry about listening to that shit – that would give us all – no, and you had several last wishes and that weren't one a the good ones, when the kids are upset-were upset and the guests are in mournin we gotta sit

	and lissen to *that* juss cos you wrote it down in a moment of 'clarity' –
A	inspiration
B	it was inappropriate
A	it was my choice
B	shit choice.
A	My last choice
B	a shit last choice.
A	
B	
A	…She hasn't shown you her cryin since my service. But, she does cry most nights most of the / night.
B	When she's ready –
A	she's ready
B	when she wants to talk to / me –
A	she's ready but she doesn't know / it.
B	I'm here. I'm always here – which is more than you are. I don't go nowhere. Don't got no one to go nowhere with. Now. Have I? I don't go out. She don't go out. He don't go nowhere. We're all here. All the time. Great. It's just, great. Here. Without you.
A	
B	And after getting it so wrong wid you, apparently *so* wrong with you, after your mum after all that, after all that tryin and after all that talkin that you said was shit and useless and wrong, after all *that* I'm now tryin to get it right. Give her space, give her time, give her the shit you wanted –
A	she's not me

B	I know-she's-not-you-I-know-she's-not-you I still want…
	I know she's not you.
A	
B	…I cry most nights.
A	
B	(I) cry every / night.
A	You're the adult.
B	I got things to say but no one to say them / to.
A	You're the adult. She's our / daughter.
B	I got things to share but no one to show them to.
A	You're grown.
B	This is / so –
A	She's our daughter
B	this is so fuckin –
A	he's our son
B	so-and-because there's nowhere I wanna go without you nuthin I wanna do without you bein / here.
A	they need / you.
B	Nights are fuckin endless and days are a disaster. That soft neck-back piece a me yearnin for that touch by you has given up waitin and gone hard and inside I gotta gap left by you bigger than my outsides –
A	y'know –
B	so if she wants to-to – to speak to me –
A	she's a child
B	I'm here but I'm / not –

A   she's the / child

B   not chasin her with words

A   she's our child

B   and-but – 'ours' has just become 'mine'. All mine
            only mine. Because of *you* – they've got each
            other thass somethin, I've not got –

A   they need their dad.

B   They got each other

A   they need their / dad.

B   I need my wife. I want my wife.

            Beat.

            I'd swap my place for your place –

A   don't.

B   …I'd swap her place for you

A   *don't*

B   to have you back and her gone.

            A *slaps him hard*.

            Both of them for one a you –

            A *slaps him harder.*
            Beat.

            Ask me again what I miss.

A

B   Ask me.

A

B   Ask me. Go on *go on*. Or would that be somethin
            that's too complex for me to understand?

A

B	I'll do a you. I'll do a sullen. I'll do a morose I'll do a silence I'll do seven – no ten months of silence I'll do that.
B	
B	
A	…They need their / dad.
B	I need my wife. I want my wife. I want my-you, back.
A	
B	You shouldn't have left me.
A	I didn't leave / you.
B	You shouldn't have left us
A	I didn't leave / you.
B	you left / us.
A	I died, I died.
B	…You left me.
A	
B	
A	And… don't let them –
B	what?
A	…Don't just let them –
B	what? 'Just let them'… what?
A	
A	You're bein –
B	what? I'm bein exactly, *what*?
A	

He gestures.

B   Name it *name* it, or would that be somethin that's
    too fuckin complex for me to understand an' all?

A

A

A

B

Scene Fourteen

A	There's enough space.
B	They been running out of space for years.
A	I booked a space had a spot booked booked a plot and I wanted to be buried.
B	I talked it over with the kids.
A	No you / didn't.
B	Talked it over with the kids and / decided –
A	No you / didn't.
B	decided – we decided that it was for the best, what they wanted was for / the –
A	no they didn't and thass not what I asked for
B	we can't always get what we ask for. Can we?
	Beat.
A	…Couldn't you be arsed with the upkeep of a headstone?
B	
A	Or the keeping-up of a plot?
B	
A	It was somewhere for the kids to come, when they wanted, when they were ready to come to, it was a place – a resting place was to be a-my resting / place.
B	The kids've lived a life of you can remember that of you don't need to go somewhere to siddown over your bones / and –
A	Not worth the plot I'd paid for? Not worth the effort of / that?
B	You're worth / it.

A	Not worth the time to trim the grass from the grave – the grave that I had paid for that I had asked for, specific, engravings that I had drawn to be designed wording that I had worked out, a headstone that I had reserved, nuthin elaborate nuthin ostentatious nuthin outrageous somethin simple somethin personal somethin tasteful and it was only a small ask to be returned to the ground, a little plot where me and you would lie side by side till / we're –
B	I aint bein buried.
A	I weren't worth / that?
B	I aint bein buried. Got no intention.
A	…You told me you would be –
B	changed my mind.
A	You said we would be –
B	toldju I changed my mind from time. If you'd listened. Bothered to lissen. Told you ages ago.
A	
B	In that straightforward way I got. Cold in the ground? No.
A	
B	
A	Prefer to be buried alone than burnt and scattered.
B	I / was –
A	You hold grudges
B	you always / said –
A	you hold grudges beyond the fuckin / grave.
B	'lissen to the kids lissen to the kids' –
A	you're bitter
B	always told me to lissen to the kids / more.

A	and don't drag the kids into your bitter shit
B	I lissen to the kids and now that's wrong as / well.
A	y'don't think I know what you're doin?
B	I'm juss –
A	you're *not* 'just' anythin and you don't have it in you y'never did – never have never will to follow fuckin… instructions. I couldn't have made it any clearer.

Beat.

God.

How-the-arse you could fuck up even my last request is – butchu managed that. An achievement a real achievement – your greatest achievement yet in y'long life of achieving fuck-all.

B	(*quietly*) Fuck you yeah.
A	(*quietly*) …Fuck, you.

Scene Fifteen

They watch each other.

Beat.

Gently she touches the back of his neck, he leans his head forward to accommodate. They are tender with each other.

He touches the back of her right thigh.

PART TWO

They are busy.

WOMAN *watches the* MAN. *He is busy. He feels her looking.*

Beat.

He continues to be busy.

WOMAN ...The thing is...
The thing is... you don't lissen. You look – like you're lookin now – you'll look like you're listening but you're not. Got no intention. But lookin like you've heard – wanting it to look like you're hearin, looking like you're hearing me.

MAN What?

WOMAN But you're not.
Is what you're doin.

He says nothing. He is busy.

Can tell can see can see it, andju know it sends me which is why y'do it – which is what *pisses* me off – if you was doin it in ignorance not outta ignorance, but in ignorance thass one thing but doin it and knowin you're doin it –.

She becomes busy.

And I lost count got tired of sayin got tired of repeatin myself bein made to repeat myself sayin how irritatin it is when you got two good ears – last time I looked – two good hearin ears thatchu choose not to use when it comes to hearin me.

He is busy.

And you do it on – doin it on purpose to make me look bad when it aint me at all it's all you, you

UNIVERSITY OF WINCHESTER LIBRARY

and your passively, pathologically, aggressively
fuckingly not-right-in-the-head bullshit version of
'listening' thatchu do. Are doin. Are doin badly.

They are busy.

MAN   …I / don't.

WOMAN   (*dry*) But iss alright.
           It's alright.

           Beat.

MAN   I don't.

WOMAN   (I) see you thinkin of doin it before you've done
           it that look that you do thass lookin at me but not
           lookin to see me –

MAN   I / don't.

WOMAN   that shit look you do where it never gets to me
           never gets that far, that far over – falters just
           beyond your eyeballs. *That.* And thinkin I don't
           notice – I notice, you don't notice I notice but
           I see it cos I look, look properly – and you're
           doin it now / your –

MAN   I'm / not.

WOMAN   your eyes are doin the equivalent of your ears.
           Vacant. Vacating the place vacating the space
           that's in between makin you look (stupid) – it
           makes you look stupid nuthin goin on behind the
           eyes – and I know you do this to get a reaction –
           get a reaction from me – iss not getting a reaction
           from me, it's not workin you need to know it's
           not workin, thought you woulda realised that by
           now an' changed your tactic – your one tactic you
           got. It don't work. Not at all. No. …And if it was
           really an apology –

MAN   it / was –

WOMAN   if it was a really proper heartfelt – properly from
           somewhere in there –

MAN   it / was –

WOMAN   from somewhere in there *meant* –

MAN   it was / you –

WOMAN   from somewhere deep down that *matters* –

MAN   it was you who should apologise to me.

            They are busy.
            Beat.

            It's you who should be apologising to / me.

WOMAN   I woulda thought about thinking of accepting it,
            that's all I'm sayin. If it was somethin from
            somewhere heartfelt from you

MAN   you sayin so much I –

WOMAN   but there was nothin to accept –

MAN   you always sayin so much that / I –

WOMAN   was there? Nuthin to (accept) – and me should be
            'apologising to you'?

MAN   You always sayin so much but not sayin nuthin –

WOMAN   I should apologise to *you*?! An' if I was *gonna*
            say / something –

MAN   I do / lissen.

WOMAN   gonna say anythin / it –

MAN   I do lissen but it's like tryin to separate the shit
            from the shovel tryin to lissen to you and I got
            nuthin to apologise for.

WOMAN   Cos you've never got nuthin to apologise for
            have you? Cos y'live life Saintly. You don't know
            how to apologise thass you, that's / your –

MAN   I don't know / how?

WOMAN   that's your problem part a your / problem.

MAN   I don't know how to apologise?

WOMAN	I thought it was-there was somethin wrong with – an illness or summink I / thought –
MAN	What are / you – ?
WOMAN	thought you had a somethin psychological – a blockage or summink – some mentally constipated something that's stopped it comin / out.
MAN	What are you talkin –?
WOMAN	But now I know it aint that
MAN	you thought I was / mental?
WOMAN	givin you too much credit –
MAN	you think I'm mental?
WOMAN	Know now there's nuthin wrong with you, know now you're just ignorant – although that is an affliction in itself –
MAN	there aint nothing wrong with / me.
WOMAN	a self-inflicted affliction like the-the lung cancer of a smoker or the diabetes of a fat fucker thass your ignorance affliction – you're a drain – drain on me like they drain on the NHS –
MAN	if I'm constipated up here (*taps head*) you're a shower of shit from there (*gestures mouth*)
WOMAN	so I don't feel sorry for you.
MAN	'Dia-fuckin-/betes'?!
WOMAN	Learned a long time ago to not bother to feel sorry for / you.
MAN	'Lung-the-fuck-/cancer'?!
WOMAN	Don't feel that, don't feel anything – just / feel –
MAN	You aint right wishing that on / me.
WOMAN	just feel pissed off mostly
MAN	you wishin that on / me?

WOMAN   just feel that now. Most of the time, pissed off.

MAN   That's fuckin –

WOMAN   andju don't *lissen* cos I didn't *wish* it on yer – did you hear me wish it on you? You did not. I'm not like that, not that kinda – it was an example y'thick fuck.

MAN   And I'm not mental

WOMAN   I was bein meta-fuckin-phorical.

MAN

WOMAN   My metaphors are lost on you.

MAN   You wouldn't know what one is

WOMAN   you clearly gotta lacka understandin – y'shoulda listened harder at school.

MAN   Woulda done if you'da shut up in class

WOMAN   O-level English –

MAN   grade C

WOMAN   takin criticism from the CSE drop-out? Don't think / so.

MAN   'Transferred use of a phrase'. Metaphor. Use it properly or not at all.

WOMAN
MAN

They are busy.

WOMAN   …(An) apology would stick in your friggin throat.

MAN   You're like the MRSA then –

WOMAN   oh we've moved / on

MAN   'metaphorically' speakin, eatin people alive –

WOMAN   moved on we've moved on and y'dunno what that is you don't even know what / that *is*.

MAN   Know that it fucks people up – affects where it
           shouldn't – outlives antibiotics and anything
           man-made – thass you – and it can't / be –

WOMAN   What does it stand for –

MAN   it can't be –

WOMAN   what does it even stand for?

MAN

MAN   It's like…

WOMAN   What does the M even stand for?

MAN

           She gestures 'go on'.
           He is busy.

WOMAN   You don't know.

           He is busy.

           So whatever that dig was meant to be didn't work
           don't work – and when have I ever had an
           apology from you?

MAN   If you shut your / mouth –

WOMAN   This the / apology?

MAN   shut your mouth and give your ears a chance –

WOMAN   that an apology? Nice.

MAN   (I) never said –

WOMAN   never faltered never failed never wronged nobody
           never wronged me never made no mistakes –

MAN   I never / said –

WOMAN   have you? Thass you. Lived the life of a fuckin
           Saint – forgot who I was talkin to there for a
           minute forgot I was talkin to Christ in the corner
           cos for a moment I thought you was just you, just
           you and your ignorant self who still aint
           apologised to / me.

MAN   I've got nuthin / to –

WOMAN   Amazing.

MAN   I never / said –

WOMAN   *Stunning. Unique* – you're unique you are –
         wish I could live like you – no conscience.
         Wish I could be like that, live life like that,
         self-centered. Selfish. Psychopathic. And 'shut
         my mouth for two minutes' – ?

MAN   Psychopathic?!

WOMAN   That's nice –

MAN   psychopathic??

WOMAN   *That's nice* that is, a nice way to talk to me. Very
         Christian, 'Christ'.

MAN   Only one psycho from where I'm / standing.

WOMAN   Thass another apology stacking up.

MAN   Must be hard bein you –

WOMAN   it's great.

MAN   Must be horrible.

WOMAN   Only horrible thing that spoils it about bein me is
         you.

MAN

WOMAN   And how you speak to me needs an apology all of
         its own.

MAN

WOMAN   And –

MAN   must be hard work keepin yourself in the state
         you're in – effort. Workin yourself up for no good
         reason – exhaustin.

WOMAN   Harder to think of others than yourself – I think
         of you – yes, that is consistently hard for me but
         I do it. Easy bein you

MAN	you don't think of me
WOMAN	you don't think of *anyone* –
MAN	consider you
WOMAN	you don't consider no one.
MAN	Consider you to stop talkin.
WOMAN	You don't consider me y'never have you ent got it in / you.
MAN	It's exhausting bein with you.
WOMAN	Piece a piss bein you in comparison to bein me.
MAN	Shit bein you.
WOMAN	Shit listening to your shit.
MAN	Shit bein with you
WOMAN	shit bein with *you*
MAN	shit havin to be with you.
WOMAN	You don't 'have to be with me' nuthin.

He pretends to be busy. She sees it.
Beat.
She is busy.

MAN	(*quietly*) …(I'm) not gonna say something I don't believe in sayin just cos –
WOMAN	what?
MAN	…I'm not gonna say something just cos you want.
WOMAN	You don't say anything I want.
MAN	I'm not / a –
WOMAN	You don't do anything I want –
MAN	don't 'do anything you / want'?
WOMAN	it's not 'anything' I'm talkin about it's '*something*'. Specifics.
MAN	I 'don't do / anything you – '

WOMAN   There's so much I could want that I trained
           myself to not. To stop. To not bother to want at
           all. Because of you.

MAN   The things I wanna do but don't cos I know you
           and know you won't, so I don't even bother say.
           All the things I'd love to do but let slide cos you –

WOMAN   all that I'd love in life, love in my / life –

MAN   let slide because of you.

WOMAN   The things I'd *love* to do in life –

MAN   you do whatchu want.

WOMAN   I do what I can.

MAN   You do exactly what you / want.

WOMAN   Do what I can, despite you.

MAN   Y'do what you do to spite me.

WOMAN   …And I don't want you to just 'say it', an
           apology needs to mean something. I need you to
           feel it and understand it and understand what it
           means to me and why you need to say it.
           Just sayin somethin don't mean nuthin.
           And I wouldn't spite you. Do somethin do
           anythin I do to 'spite you'.
           Thass a sign of you – *that's* a sign of how you're
           takin it if you're takin it / like that.

MAN   I take it how it's given –

WOMAN   now you're just talkin shit.

MAN   (*dry*) Nice.

WOMAN   I am.
           Y'need to apologise

MAN   if it don't need to be said –

WOMAN   I feel it needs to be said.

MAN   You feel everything needs to be / said.

WOMAN	What I feel matters –
MAN	you feel every fuckin thing matters thass the problem –
WOMAN	just apologise.
MAN	You over-talk y'know that?
WOMAN	Apologise
MAN	y'never stop and the fact is you *feel* I need to apologise. I *feel* I don't.
WOMAN	…You aint got no feelings.
MAN	Oh. Right. Mature.
WOMAN	You don't feel.
MAN	Not like you.
WOMAN	Couldn't feel like / me.
MAN	Don't wanna feel like you
WOMAN	(you) don't feel me, no
MAN	cos you feel hard.
WOMAN	Long time since you were.
MAN	Wonder why that is?
WOMAN	I stopped wondering with you a long time / ago.
MAN	You don't want a man, you want / a –
WOMAN	Still lookin for the man in / you.
MAN	you want a version of you with a dick.
WOMAN	That'd be nice.
MAN	You want a self-help book-of-shit tellin you what you wanna hear – you want a robot with a dick that don't answer back –
WOMAN	something with a dick would be nice –
MAN	my dick would like something nice

WOMAN	y'dick must be dusty haven't seen it for so / long.
MAN	lacka excitement it's bored you bore it and it aint been hard cos you're hard to get hard for.
WOMAN	
MAN	What?
WOMAN	

She is not busy enough.

| MAN | …What? |

Beat.

WOMAN	…Y'don't hurt y'know, you don't hurt me – that / kinda –
MAN	(I'm) not tryin to hurt / you.
WOMAN	that kinda… sayin that kinda… it don't hurt me / y'know.
MAN	Not trying to hurt you just stating a fact. Fact. Thass how I feel.

He tries to stay busy.

Seein as we talkin bout how we 'feelin'.

She watches him.
He stops being busy.

MAN
WOMAN

She starts being busy again. Not busy enough.
Beat.

WOMAN   (*quietly*) …The reason I wouldn't recognise an apology from you is cos I aint never heard one. Aint never had one. Never. Not once. Not a half word, not a whisper in the wind, nuthin.

And if you wanna start with one, there's a *really* good reason to start now.

MAN

>*Beat*.

WOMAN

>*Beat*.
>
>(*quietly*) …Right.

MAN

WOMAN   …Be a shock getting an apology from you. Cause me a condition.

MAN   Comin from you.

WOMAN   Bring me out in sweats or summink

MAN   if you're gonna have a turn have one quietly, lemme know when you're done and I'll scrape up what's left of yer.

WOMAN   …Oh. Nice. Nice. You'd just stand and watch.

MAN   I'm busy.

WOMAN   Would let me suffer.

MAN   I'm / busy.

WOMAN   Like you did before –

MAN   you weren't suffering.

WOMAN   I have to get to suffering before I get a reaction from / you?

MAN   You weren't (suffering) even how you talk, even how you – 'suffering'? You were under-the-weather.

WOMAN   I was ill.

MAN   Y'felt a bit rough

WOMAN   that what you call / it?

MAN   thass what *you* called it. You 'felt rough' you said –

WOMAN	what I said don't matter when you could see that I was – you could see I weren't right. Normal people would see and say something.
MAN	I said to you that you didn't look right –
WOMAN	you said it once.
MAN	You said to me 'you felt a bit under-the-fuckin-weather is / all'.
WOMAN	You said it / once.
MAN	I said it once cos I *lissen* – I heard you. And respecting what you say –'said', I took you at your word.
WOMAN	
MAN	And I was there and I stayed / there –
WOMAN	Must've been ill for you to / do that
MAN	stayed there and never left your side –
WOMAN	to 'respect what I / said'.
MAN	couldn't leave your side never left your side cos I could *see* something weren't right with you.
	Beat.
WOMAN	…You was there in body not mind and sat there resentful.
MAN	(*quietly*) For fuck's / sake.
WOMAN	Could feel it. Vacant and resentful
MAN	I was / there.
WOMAN	be better you not bein there.
MAN	I stayed / there.
WOMAN	Felt bad about feelin bad havin you sittin there with your awful aura in the room. Bad airs, bad air, bad aura.
MAN	

WOMAN   You didn't even ask how I was feeling.

MAN   I *knew* how you was 'feelin'. Fuck. I could *see* it.

           …And a thank you for changing your sheets
           woulda been nice
           and a thank you for spoonfeeding you
           and a thank you for lifting fresh water to your lips
           and a thank you for cooling your fever
           and a thank you for easing your shakes,
           a thank you for takin out the sick bucket – for
           takin out the shit bucket,
           a thank you was it for cleaning you gently and
           thank you again for redressing your dressings
           gentler than they did and a thank you for – I could
           go on.

WOMAN
MAN

MAN   …And a final thank you, for not sayin how fuckin
           frightened I was.

           I should wait for that 'thank you' from back then
           should I? Or I should wait for an apology from
           you now…?

WOMAN

MAN   …You tell me how long I should wait.

           Beat.

WOMAN   (*quietly*) …If I took a turn again. I'd turn to you.

           Beat.
           Pause.

           I would.

           *They both become busy. She can't sustain her
           business.*

WOMAN

           Beat.

MAN   What?

WOMAN	
MAN	What?
WOMAN	Nothing.
	Beat.
	(*quietly*) …I know how frightened you were.
	Beat.
MAN	(*quietly*) …Knew how frightened you were.
WOMAN	
MAN	
	He nods, just.
WOMAN	(*quietly*) I was –.
WOMAN	
MAN	
WOMAN	I do…
MAN	what?
WOMAN	
MAN	What?
	She becomes busy again.
WOMAN	(I) do want to say…
	She doesn't continue.
MAN	…Whatever.
WOMAN	
WOMAN	If you would just say –
MAN	a thank you shouldn't come with no conditions.
WOMAN	It's not no condition –
MAN	from there's a 'just' and a 'you' in there, there's a condition.
WOMAN	

MAN	'A thing that must exist if something else is to exist or occur'. Condition. By definition.
WOMAN	A figure of speech.
MAN	(*dry*) A metaphor?

Beat.

I wannit unconditional.

WOMAN	That's a condition of your own.

…You do still owe me an / apology.

MAN	You're doin terms and conditions now
WOMAN	I'm-we're not-I'm not…
MAN	
WOMAN	

Beat.

WOMAN	…If you say what you need to say to me first
MAN	first?
WOMAN	I didn't mean –
MAN	'*first*'? Terms, conditions and a timetable. / Shit.
WOMAN	I meant, 'as well'. I meant…
MAN	
WOMAN	I meant –.
MAN	
WOMAN	…I didn't mean that. Like that.

Beat.

WOMAN	

Beat.

MAN	…Howdju want me? All ears?

She is uncomfortable.

Seated?

Stood?
Eyes on yer, eyes away, what? Nuthin vacant.
Looking, all the way over?

WOMAN   Don't take the piss.

MAN
WOMAN

MAN   (*quietly*) I'm not.

Pause.

WOMAN   And I'm… we've got a –. (*she gestures*)

If I do, you do.

He gestures back, a little ambiguously.
Silence.

…

…I just wanna say…

then…

She exhales quietly.

MAN

WOMAN   …Thank…

Thank you.

MAN
WOMAN

WOMAN   And…

Sorry.

Beat.
He nods, just.
Beat.
She nods back, just.

MAN
WOMAN

She gestures to him.

MAN
WOMAN

She gestures for him to say something.

MAN

MAN

Silence, for as long as it can be held.

PART THREE

MAN   Nothin.

     The YOUNG WOMAN *isn't particularly*
     listening to him.

Y. WOMAN

MAN   Nothing about you.

Y. WOMAN

MAN   Nothing about you to change. You know that?
     I wouldn't change nothing about – nuthin about
     you could be better.

     Beat.

     You know that?

Y. WOMAN What?

MAN   Wouldn't change a thing.

Y. WOMAN

MAN   Wouldn't wanna change anything.

     He smiles.
     Beat.

     About you.

     Beat.

     …Me?

Y. WOMAN What?

     He gestures.

     What.

MAN   …Would you change anything about…

The YOUNG WOMAN *isn't paying attention.*
Beat.

Wouldn't change even a little thing about you…
but…

He watches her. She feels it.

Y. WOMAN   What?

He gestures 'me'?
Beat.
She isn't particularly paying attention.

MAN   Don't matter.

Beat.

…You should talk to him.

Y. WOMAN

MAN   You should, I think, that's all I'm…

Y. WOMAN

MAN   You should talk to / him.

Y. WOMAN   I talk.

MAN   You should talk to him properly it's obvious it's –

Y. WOMAN   (*dry*) I 'should talk to him'

MAN   obvious it's on your mind –

Y. WOMAN   it's not.

MAN   Playin on your / mind.

Y. WOMAN   He's not.

MAN   Y'look like you wanna talk to him.

Y. WOMAN   I don't.

MAN   …You do.

Y. WOMAN   I do know what I look like and I don't look like
             I want to talk to –

MAN   you're not lookin at you I am – and iss lovely –
               and you do look like –

Y. WOMAN   I don't and –

MAN   you've looked like that for weeks

Y. WOMAN   I've talked to / him.

MAN   you've looked like this for months.

Y. WOMAN   I've talked at him for years tried with him for /
               years.

MAN   Do you good to say somethin.

Y. WOMAN   You do me good.

MAN   Not good enough by the look of / it.

Y. WOMAN   You do great you do me great. It's great – what.

               Beat.

MAN   …Talk to him –

               *She goes to say something, before she can he
               continues.*

               not for him to nuthin-about-him but for you to
               feel better for you / then.

Y. WOMAN   'Feel better for me'?

MAN   Make it about –

Y. WOMAN   I need to 'feel better' for / me?

MAN   make it about you is what I –

Y. WOMAN   is that what I look like an' / all?

MAN   is what I mean. / It –

Y. WOMAN   I 'look like' I need to feel better about it is it?
               That I 'look like' I need to feel better about him?

MAN   It wasn't –

Y. WOMAN   I've tried talkin to / him.

MAN   it sounds selfish but –

Y. WOMAN   I've tried talkin / to –

MAN   talk how you talk, / talk –

Y. WOMAN   talking to him / doesn't –

MAN   talk how you talk to me to him, you don't stop
             talkin to me – in a good way, y'never shut up.
             In a good way –

Y. WOMAN   which you –

MAN   which is what I like. Love. Bit of what I like
             amongst the lot of what I love. About you.
             Y'know that. But be selfish – if you have to, talk
             to him to get what you need to feel better about –

Y. WOMAN   I don't need to talk to him to 'feel better about'
             anything, I got nuthin to feel better about – I feel
             fine and talkin to him wouldn't be how to make
             me feel better if I didn't.

Y. WOMAN

MAN   Love you talkin. Y'know that.

Y. WOMAN   I know / that.

MAN   Love how you talk –

Y. WOMAN   I / know.

MAN   love that it's non-stop. Love your lovely noise in
             my ears. All the time.

             She smiles, says nothing. He sees.

             Hmmm.

             He kisses her lightly.

             …And me?

             She is distracted.

Y. WOMAN

MAN   …Anything about me…? That you (love)…

Y. WOMAN

MAN   (I) like how you wake up with words – your
               words. Bathe with a dialogue and breakfast with a
               chat. Like how you go to work missing me, call
               me up on your way. Like how you talk quiet when
               you're outside in public on the phone to / me –

Y. WOMAN   You said –

MAN   like how you text me when you can't talk and –

Y. WOMAN   you said / it –

MAN   and-and FaceTime me in your first break.

Y. WOMAN   You said it got on your nerves.

MAN   Like how on your lunch break you'd –

Y. WOMAN   (you) said I got on your / nerves.

MAN   find the time to phone and say the right – not 'on
               my nerves' –

Y. WOMAN   'on your last nerve'

MAN   I was havin a – only said that when – I was bein-
               havin a-a-… no. Not on my nerves. You don't –

Y. WOMAN   did sometimes.

MAN   Y'didn't.

Y. WOMAN   Do sometimes

MAN   I –

Y. WOMAN   sometimes you say to me –

MAN   on occasion I might have said –

Y. WOMAN   say to me

MAN   on an occasion I might have said somethin when
               sometimes I weren't in the right – sometimes I get
               in my – y'know –

Y. WOMAN   moods

MAN	sometimes y'know –
Y. WOMAN	moods
MAN	that I get up in my – a bit and
Y. WOMAN	moody
MAN	and stay there. Too long. Till you talk me out of it. Like you do like only you do, can do.
Y. WOMAN	
MAN	…But, 'moody' I dunno if I would – don't think I would quite… y'know, (put it) like that.
Y. WOMAN	I'd change that –
MAN	'moods' is a / bit –
Y. WOMAN	change that about yer
MAN	'moody' is a bit strong –
Y. WOMAN	change that about you in a minute.

Beat.

MAN	…Talk to him. He's your dad.
Y. WOMAN	He won't talk to me about you.
MAN	Talk about somethin else / then.
Y. WOMAN	I wanna talk about you talk about me and you
MAN	talk about what he wants to talk about.
Y. WOMAN	Thass not a conversation
MAN	that's not a conversation about what you want, but iss something.
Y. WOMAN	Thass him controlling the subject
MAN	that's you engaging with him.
Y. WOMAN	He talks about nothing
MAN	let him talk about anything.
Y. WOMAN	He talks about anything but me

MAN   listen to what he wants to talk / about then.

Y. WOMAN   he doesn't talk. I end up listenin to he's sighs and
             shit efforts and his silence again, I want him to talk
             like he used to talk like he talked before Mum…
             and then there was after Mum. When I thought
             there was no after. And he's had years to get over
             that, years to get back to talkin how he did before,
             years to stop turning up his TV too loud tryinta
             mask he's tears over that and-when-and-and he's
             never listened to me. Ever listened to me.

             He kisses her.

MAN   (It) won't hurt to try again

Y. WOMAN   he thinks you're too old for me.

MAN   I am too old for you.

Y. WOMAN   (He) said old men are temperamental

MAN   'old' I wouldn't / say –

Y. WOMAN   said they don't know what they want, unless it's
             something new and shiny.

MAN   Knew I wanted you, was / sure.

Y. WOMAN   That is somethin he does say – one of the only
             things he does / say.

MAN   Given him somethin to talk about then –

Y. WOMAN   thinks there's somethin wrong with you going out
             with someone as young as me.

MAN   Seems to say a lot for someone who don't say
             much. He's, obviously still got opinions

Y. WOMAN   still got somethin to say about / that

MAN   well –

Y. WOMAN   will only talk about that will only talk about you
             in that way, has always talked about you in that
             way so we end up – we always end up, y'know…

MAN

Y. WOMAN   …And 'tryin' – me tryin, does. '…Hurt.'

Y. WOMAN

> MAN *kisses her gently.*

MAN   He's older than me.

Y. WOMAN   What?

MAN   He's older'n me.

Y. WOMAN   Not much.

MAN   He's – there are a few years in between –

Y. WOMAN   not enough. He says

MAN   well

Y. WOMAN   not by much at all. He says. And then he's silent again. It's not even a argument, I have my say he shuts up – I'm arguing with silence his silence, again, then that shuts me up.

MAN   …Talk to your brother about talking to him.

Y. WOMAN   He thinks I'm too young for you.

MAN   …You are.

> *He kisses her again.*

Y. WOMAN   He don't know what's wrong with me going out with someone as old as you.

MAN   Right.

Y. WOMAN   Goin out with someone as old as you for as long as I have.

MAN   Right

Y. WOMAN   he thinks I lost my mind (he) thinks I'm goin through a phase – thought I was going through a phase – thinks it's linked to Dad in some way (and) tries to psycho something about me says I got psychologicals –

MAN   right

Y. WOMAN   says you're gettin more out of this than I am –

MAN   okay / that's –

Y. WOMAN   he thinks there's some trophy su'un going on
             somewhere with you and thinks we've got nothing
             to say that can cross the age gap to say it in.

MAN   …Right.

Y. WOMAN   Thinks I'm missing out on life not seeing
             someone my own age.
             Yeh.
             Me and my brother talk.

MAN   …Your brother talks a lot.

Y. WOMAN   And after Mum…

MAN   I know

Y. WOMAN   you don't

MAN   I know that must –

Y. WOMAN   no you don't. After Mum was…

MAN   …Talk to your brother about that.

Y. WOMAN

MAN   I know.

Y. WOMAN   You don't.

             He kisses her.

             Scattered to the four fuckin winds which is what
             she wanted, Dad said.
             Feel a breeze think of Mum. Dad said.
             Feel a breeze… and I don't feel nothin. But cold.

MAN   …Talk to your brother –

Y. WOMAN   I think she would have wanted a grave. I want
             a grave-would want a grave when – whenever –

MAN   I'd come and tend it –

Y. WOMAN   you're older than me you'd go before me I'd be tending yours.

MAN   …Talk to your brother about your –

Y. WOMAN   my brother only wants to talk about you.

MAN

Y. WOMAN   And the wrong decisions I'm makin – he thinks I'm makin.

MAN   …Right.

Y. WOMAN   And the fuckin up of my life he thinks I'm –

MAN   maybe your brother –

Y. WOMAN   thinks I still am doin

MAN   maybe your brother / isn't –

Y. WOMAN   pointin out what I'll regret what he thinks I'll regret by bein with / you

MAN   your brother isn't the best / person to –

Y. WOMAN   and you said I talk to my brother too much you said you wanted me to talk to you, you wanted me to talk to you more – you wanted me to talk to you as much as I talked to my brother.
And my brother won't talk to me as much as he did cos he only wants to talk about me and you which I ent talking about no more. To him. But he's got plenty still to say about what he thinks, of me.
Got even more to say bout what he thinks of you. So I talk to you, talk to you as much as I talked to him and then you tell me you can't take it. You tell me that I should learn to listen learn to be quiet which I learnt for most of my years with Dad after Mum and that. After all that. My talkin has started to get on your nerves 'got on your last nerve'. You said. Have said. Moody or not moody.

   Beat.

MAN   …I might have said that once…

Y. WOMAN	more than once.
MAN	On the way back from seeing her or something
Y. WOMAN	more than once and you –
MAN	she puts me in a – she punishes me with her moods.
Y. WOMAN	You've said it when you haven't been and don't go. Don't go, if it's that –
MAN	I don't wanna go
Y. WOMAN	don't go if / it's –
MAN	I don't wanna go but I go, should go cos –
Y. WOMAN	you don't owe her anything.
MAN	I go cos it's decent. I go cos she's not well.
Y. WOMAN	Again.
MAN	She's not been well
Y. WOMAN	again.
MAN	She's / not –
Y. WOMAN	She's not your responsibility.
MAN	She's not my responsibility.
Y. WOMAN	No.
MAN	I go and when I go I talk about you, that pisses her off
Y. WOMAN	shouldn't go at / all.
MAN	I go to be decent, go to see she's alright, see she's alright talk about you, piss her off and leave.
Y. WOMAN	She's not as sick as she says she / is.
MAN	I go. I check on her. We sit down. She makes a bitter brew (of tea), I don't stop talkin about you, she bangs down the kettle and doesn't offer me a drink. I tell her how great you are. She clatters open the cupboard and avoids eye contact, (I) tell

her how great bein with you is – she throws hot
water into her mug – still not offering me mine in
mine, and I count off the good years of bein with
you. She sugars her hot drink – too many to
count, while I think of you. She slices her latest
bake effort not offering me none, while I look at
her and wish it was you. She sits down heavy –
face like thunder sips on her hot drink halfway
eats her cake watching my mind wander on to
you, when she says what she says –

Y. WOMAN   your own / mug?

MAN   says what she always says –

Y. WOMAN   you have your / own –

MAN   says about herself goes on about herself –

Y. WOMAN   how have / you –

MAN   sayin it tight through her teeth clenched tight –

Y. WOMAN   you have your own mug round there?

MAN   What?

Y. WOMAN   Your own mug.

MAN   She –

Y. WOMAN   you.

MAN   What?

MAN
Y. WOMAN

    She half-laughs a little.

    (*dry*) Whatever.

MAN   …When she talks she doesn't talk like you. When
we laugh she don't laugh like you, when we –

Y. WOMAN   (*dry*) she bakes for –

MAN   when we watch what we watch she don't watch
what you / would.

Y. WOMAN   she bakes for you.

MAN   She bakes.

Y. WOMAN   (*dry*) You gotta special plate?

MAN   Are you – ?

Y. WOMAN   Are *you*?

MAN   …She says you're 'lucky to have me'.

Y. WOMAN   Are you / that –

MAN   Says 'you don't know how lucky you are'

Y. WOMAN   you that / gullible?

MAN   says I'm unique – well, actually says I'm 'fuckin unique'

Y. WOMAN   or just that / stupid?

MAN   then goes into all her metaphorical shit that was always borin and how she's happy to be not disappointed no more, so I make a brew myself and sort myself / out.

Y. WOMAN   She's not sick.

MAN   She is.

Y. WOMAN   Not as sick as she –

MAN   she / is.

Y. WOMAN   and I'd change that. Change that about you. Change that about you bein so gullible.

MAN   She's old.

Y. WOMAN   You're old.

MAN   …You jealous?

Y. WOMAN   Nuthin to be jealous of knowin you don't date old (people) – people your own age.

MAN
Y. WOMAN

          Beat.

Y. WOMAN   (*dry*) Make a brew in your own mug do yer?

MAN   …So you catch me in a mood and maybe you
           catch me in a mood comin back from that, comin
           back from her and I might say somethin sharp
           I don't mean.

Y. WOMAN   You've said it more than –

MAN   and I'm not counting – you counting you doin
           that?

Y. WOMAN   I'm just –

MAN   thass kinda –

Y. WOMAN   was / just

MAN   kinda a little bit juvenile. If you're doing that.
           Counting up the times –

Y. WOMAN   countin up your moods?

MAN   Really. A bit childish.

Y. WOMAN

MAN   Are you doing that?

Y. WOMAN

MAN   Stackin your grudges against me?

Y. WOMAN

MAN   Are yer?

Y. WOMAN   This isn't –

MAN   are yer? Cos if we're countin –

Y. WOMAN   this isn't / that.

MAN   I could count up your silences –

Y. WOMAN   this isn't –

MAN   could count up your silences with your mind
           wandering on to y'mum or y'dysfunctional –

Y. WOMAN   don't talk about / my –

MAN   well I couldn't count would lose count and
               wouldn't count up anyway cos that is a bit...
               isn't it. I don't do that.

Y. WOMAN

MAN   Y'know I don't do that. Don't hold grudges, don't
               count grudges don't stack em up. Like you are –.

Y. WOMAN   ...I don't –

MAN   like you're doin

Y. WOMAN   this isn't that.

MAN   You are you are –

Y. WOMAN   I'm –

MAN   you're holding grudges

Y. WOMAN   I'm not

MAN   yes you –

Y. WOMAN   I'm / not.

MAN   say if you are, I mean, y'know –

Y. WOMAN   I / would.

MAN   y'know –

Y. WOMAN   I would say

MAN   say it if you mean it –

Y. WOMAN   I wouldn't not / say.

MAN   and if I've y'know – it's that upsetting to you –

Y. WOMAN   I'm not upset

MAN   if it affects you that much to the point where
               you're –

Y. WOMAN   your gullibility doesn't upset me

MAN   if I'm upsetting you to the point you're holding
               grudges against me – and it's not – I'm *not* /
               gullible.

Y. WOMAN you dunno whatchu / are.

MAN   if me seein my sick friend makes you / so –

Y. WOMAN and I'm not 'upset'

MAN   seein my sick / friend –

Y. WOMAN y'think this is an 'upset' look is it? Gullibility –

MAN   I'm / *not* –

Y. WOMAN doesn't upset me and she wasn't just your 'friend'
          and you doin whatever 'tea and biscuits' y'doin
          round there doesn't make me anythin

MAN   it makes you somethin you holdin it against me it
          obviously makes you feel / something.

Y. WOMAN Nuthin obvious about me

MAN   and it's cake

Y. WOMAN what?

MAN   She don't do biscuits.

Y. WOMAN (*quietly*) Fuck / off.

MAN   You're obviously pissed off

Y. WOMAN no.

MAN   Yeah you are –

Y. WOMAN no.

MAN   I know what your 'pissed off' looks like. I do
          know that. Had plenty of…

          She shakes her head.

Y. WOMAN

MAN   …(*dry*) Another silence.

Y. WOMAN
MAN

          Beat.
          He kisses her gently.

MAN	Want me to apologise?
Y. WOMAN	
MAN	Want me to –
Y. WOMAN	y'don't apologise.
MAN	Want me to say –
Y. WOMAN	you never / apologise.
MAN	if you want that, if that would make you feel –
Y. WOMAN	have never apologised. Never apologised to / me.
MAN	if that would get you outta your 'mood' if that's what you need to hear to make you feel…
Y. WOMAN MAN	
Y. WOMAN	…Y'know… I say so much, have to say so much – to you – cos I'm not sure it's gone in. I'm not sure that you get it that you got it. I can't tell if you've heard it, if you've wanted to hear it. If you've listened. To me at all.
MAN	I love hearing / your –
Y. WOMAN	It's not easy to tell with you with that look thatchu do, that one where y' look like y'listenin, like you've heard, but your glazed look that you're doin now never actually gets over far enough for me to-to… it is hard to tell.
MAN	…If you want me to –
Y. WOMAN	it's not about apologising – if I get on your nerves –
MAN	I can –
Y. WOMAN	if my talkin gets on your nerves
MAN	it was only
Y. WOMAN	no it wasn't, but thass alright.

Y. WOMAN

MAN

MAN   I wouldn't have you no other way you know /
           that.

Y. WOMAN   Thass what I told my brother.

MAN   Nuthin I would change about you.

Y. WOMAN   Thass what I told my dad.

MAN   I'm not askin you to change

Y. WOMAN   I know I know.

MAN   I love you.

Y. WOMAN   I know.

MAN   Love everything about you.

Y. WOMAN   (I) know that too.

MAN   Even though you do talk a lot but that's just a –

Y. WOMAN   you not lissenin I would change / that.

MAN   thass just a minor thing

Y. WOMAN   I would change that about you

MAN   but I wouldn't change nuthin of / you.

Y. WOMAN   Change your gaze of a look thatchu do, would get
           rid of that.

           Beat.

           Change your hard-edged sighs when I haven't
           even finished a sentence.
           …Would change that.

           Beat.
           She kisses him.

           Change your you kissin me to not solve nuthin –
           would change that.

Change you bringin back cake from hers would change that.
Change how you snap at me –

MAN   (I) don't snap at / you.

Y. WOMAN   yeh y'do would change that quick-time. Change you askin about you to / me –

MAN   Maybe juss a tweak –

Y. WOMAN   shit thass annoyin would change that would change your raised eyes of when you're bored of what / I'm sayin.

MAN   a tweak to the amount of talkin thatchu / do –

Y. WOMAN   Change how you talk about my dad – would / change –

MAN   a slight amend on the endlessness of / that.

Y. WOMAN   change your attitude and your tone / generally.

MAN   Maybe more than an amend

Y. WOMAN   change your moods in a minute –

MAN   cos that bit about you talkin –

Y. WOMAN   change all a them an' there's plenty a them / to change.

MAN   – and I'm not moody but that bit about you talkin does need that. A change to that – a change about that. That does get irritatin. Is more than irritatin – does my head in you doin that. Sittin wistful about your dad and lookin miserable about y'brother – would change (that) – and yeah y'do look like that which is all the time half the time. Would change that. Ignorin me – which y'do –

Y. WOMAN

MAN   see!

Y. WOMAN

MAN   (You) do on purpose would change that about you

She ignores him.

the endless phone calls of insecurity and texts of
drama – all of that would change – FaceTime –
what is the point? You lookin exactly how you're
feelin not maskin nuthin not able to mask nuthin
– get them looks for free when I'm with you
don't need to see it on no phone, that could
change cos you could make the effort. If you
could be arsed. Your endless reportin of what
your fucked-up family don't never say – would
love to change that about you – you talkin *at* me,
you talkin at me –.
All the time like that.
All the time.
That does need changin.
Would properly change that.
About you.
If you could change that.
About you.
For me.
Change that. Do that, some a that – all a that.
Some a them – all a them.
That would… that would –.
Would be…
That would be…

Beat.

They kiss.

Thass all.

End.

Other Titles in this Series

A Nick Hern Book

a profoundly affectionate, passionate devotion to someone (– noun) first published
in Great Britain in 2017 as a paperback original by Nick Hern Books Limited,
The Glasshouse, 49a Goldhawk Road, London W12 8QP, in association with
the Royal Court Theatre

a profoundly affectionate, passionate devotion to someone (– noun) copyright
© 2017 debbie tucker green

debbie tucker green has asserted her right to be identified as the author of
this work

Cover image: Root

Designed and typeset by Nick Hern Books, London
Printed in Great Britain by CPI Group (UK) Ltd

A CIP catalogue record for this book is available from the British Library

ISBN 978 1 84842 637 5

CAUTION   All rights whatsoever in this play are strictly reserved. Requests
to reproduce the text in whole or in part should be addressed to the publisher.

Amateur Performing Rights   Applications for performance, including
readings and excerpts, by amateurs in the English language throughout the
world should be addressed to the Performing Rights Manager, Nick Hern
Books, The Glasshouse, 49a Goldhawk Road, London W12 8QP,
tel +44 (0)20 8749 4953, *email* rights@nickhernbooks.co.uk, except as follows:

Australia: Dominie Drama, 8 Cross Street, Brookvale 2100, *tel* (2) 9938 8686,
fax (2) 9938 8695, *email* drama@dominie.com.au

New Zealand: Play Bureau, PO Box 9013, St Clair, Dunedin 9047,
tel (3) 455 9959, *email* info@playbureau.com

South Africa: DALRO (pty) Ltd, PO Box 31627, 2017 Braamfontein,
tel (11) 712 8000, *fax* (11) 403 9094, *email* theatricals@dalro.co.za

United States of America and Canada: The Agency (London) Ltd, see details
below

Professional Performing Rights   Applications for performance by
professionals in any medium and in any language throughout the world (and
amateur and stock performances in the United States of America and Canada)
should be addressed to The Agency (London) Ltd, 24 Pottery Lane, Holland Park,
London W11 4LZ, *fax* +44 (0)20 7727 9037, *email* info@theagency.co.uk

No performance of any kind may be given unless a licence has been obtained.
Applications should be made before rehearsals begin. Publication of this play does
not necessarily indicate its availability for amateur performance.

MIX
Paper from
responsible sources
FSC
www.fsc.org   **FSC® C013604**

UNIVERSITY OF WINCHESTER

www.nickhernbooks.co.uk

 facebook.com/nickhernbooks

twitter.com/nickhernbooks